MS. GLORIA STEINEM

A LIFE

MS. GLORIA STEINEM

A LIFE

WINIFRED CONKLING

SQUARE
FISH

FEIWEL AND FRIENDS

NEW YORK

SQUARE
FISH

An imprint of Macmillan Publishing Group, LLC
120 Broadway, New York, NY 10271 • fiercereads.com

Square Fish and the Square Fish logo are trademarks of Macmillan and are used by Feiwel and Friends under license from Macmillan.

Our books may be purchased in bulk for promotional, educational, or business use. Please contact your local bookseller or the Macmillan Corporate and Premium Sales Department at (800) 221-7945 ext. 5442 or by email at MacmillanSpecialMarkets@macmillan.com.

Library of Congress Cataloging-in-Publication Data is available.

Originally published in the United States by Feiwel and Friends
First Square Fish edition, 2022
Book designed by Liz Dresner
Square Fish logo designed by Filomena Tuosto
Printed in the United States of America.

ISBN 978-1-250-83304-4 (paperback)
10 9 8 7 6 5 4 3 2 1

LEXILE: 1110L

For my mother, Sarah Pamelia Leech Conkling, MD

You left before meeting the next generation;
your granddaughters would make you proud.

CONTENTS

A portrait of Gloria Steinem published in the 1956 Smith
College yearbook, *The Hamper*
[Smith College]

CHAPTER 1

ALMOST

Once you get a taste of being independent, you'll never want to get married.

—RUTH STEINEM

When she was twenty-two years old, Gloria Steinem almost said "I do."

In the fall of 1955, Steinem reluctantly agreed to allow a friend from college to set her up on a blind date. While visiting a girlfriend's family in Westchester County, New York, Steinem went out with Blair Chotzinoff, a handsome pilot for the Air National Guard in Purchase, New York.

The two hit it off. Chotzinoff later said that he knew within five minutes that he was going to ask Steinem to marry him. He fell for her intellect and energy, her adventurous spirit and openness to life. Steinem was smitten, too. She had had plenty of boyfriends, but Chotzinoff was different: He was seven years older, a bit of a rebel, and the chemistry between them was undeniable.

At the end of the weekend, Chotzinoff impressed Steinem by renting a four-passenger plane and flying her back to Northampton, Massachusetts. Steinem was exposed to wealth and privilege while at Smith College, and she was certainly aware of the status and security she could achieve by marrying a man who offered social and financial stability. From that point on, the couple spent almost every weekend together, either in New York or Massachusetts. Chotzinoff announced his love by piloting a small jet with an afterburner and writing *Gloria* across the sky above the Smith campus.

Steinem admired the Chotzinoff family and imagined herself a part of it. Blair came from a musical family—his uncle was a world-famous violinist, his father was a gifted pianist, and his mother had appeared in a Broadway musical. The family wasn't wealthy, but they socialized with well-known musicians from all over the world. Chotzinoff wrote a restaurant column for the *New York Post*, having worked his way up from being a copy boy.

The following spring, Steinem accepted a diamond ring from Chotzinoff. She agreed to marry because that's what she thought she was *supposed* to do. A few weeks later, she called him in tears, explaining that she couldn't see herself as a bride—or a wife. It wasn't that she didn't love him—she did—but she didn't want to define herself and her life through her relationship to a man, any man. Chotzinoff drove up to see her and after several hours of crying and talking, Steinem changed her mind and again agreed to marry him.

But it still felt wrong. Steinem considered marriage an end and not a beginning. She considered marriage "a little death. Because it's the last choice you can make." According to the conventions of the 1950s, a wife was expected to devote herself to her husband and children. Even in a happy relationship, a woman would be defined by her marriage and her service to others. Steinem wanted a life of her own.

Steinem was skeptical about the myth of happily ever after. Her childhood experiences had taught her to question the idea that women obtained personal and financial security through marriage. Steinem had watched her mother struggle to surrender herself to the needs and desires of her husband and children. Ultimately, her mother was left poor and alone: When her parents divorced, it was ten-year-old Gloria who was left to spend the next seven years taking care of her mentally ill mother. During this time in her childhood, Steinem learned firsthand what it was like to be a caregiver, putting the needs of her mother before her own. Unlike many women of her generation, who expected to find security through marriage, Steinem believed in independence and self-reliance. She was afraid of being trapped by duty and obligation.

As it turned out, Steinem wasn't the only one who had reservations about the marriage. Chotzinoff's parents questioned if she was the right match for their son. Her future father-in-law didn't like Steinem's outspokenness or her willingness to challenge him in conversation. He wanted his son to marry a traditional woman, one who would be more likely to play the conventional role of wife and mother. Knowing it would upset her, Chotzinoff's father told Steinem that he was going to give her cookware for a wedding present so that she could make him his favorite beef stew.

Steinem faced an agonizing decision. She questioned the idea of marriage but not her passion for Chotzinoff. "I loved him and cared about him and had discovered sex with him, and I didn't want to leave," Steinem said. "And I felt I had no life of my own. So I was just totally confused." She couldn't imagine a future with him—or without him. At that point in her life, she was just beginning to experience her freedom as an independent adult, and she didn't want to give it up.

Days and months slipped away. Steinem graduated from Smith in June 1956 and spent the summer with her mother in Washington, DC, planning the wedding and traveling frequently to New York to look for an apartment and a job. Steinem's mother, Ruth, liked Chotzinoff and thought that her daughter could be content as a wife, but she did make a revealing statement when Gloria was struggling to find work. "It's probably a good idea if you get married right out of college," Ruth Steinem told her daughter, "because once you get a taste of being independent, you'll never want to get married."

Steinem couldn't go through with it. In the late summer she went to New York and spent one last night with Chotzinoff. In the early morning, she slipped the engagement ring off her finger and left it on his bedside table with a note explaining that she couldn't go through with the marriage. She snuck away while he was still asleep.

After he found the note, Chotzinoff reached out to Steinem, but she didn't respond. Instead, she accepted a postgraduate fellowship to study and travel in India. She wanted to get away because she didn't trust herself to resist Chotzinoff if she saw him again.

It's impossible to know what might have been, but if Steinem had chosen to marry Chotzinoff, she may never have changed the world the way she did. By breaking with traditional expectations, Steinem was able to realize her dreams and redefine what it meant to be a twentieth-century feminist. She became a respected journalist and author; she cofounded *Ms.* magazine and wrote a half-dozen bestselling books. She became a political activist and social reformer; she cofounded the National Women's Political Caucus, the Ms. Foundation, and the Women's Media Center, among other groups. She became a leader in the women's movement, raising her voice and speaking out on feminist issues for decades. In 2013, Barack Obama awarded Steinem the Presidential Medal of Freedom, the highest nonmilitary honor given by the United States government, and she has been included in a number of lists of the most influential women in America.

What made Steinem change her mind and turn down Chotzinoff's proposal? What gave her the confidence to resist the social pressures of her day to marry and lead a traditional life? While there is no single answer, her choices reflect some of the formative experiences of her childhood.

The Steinem family
[Jess Magoo]

CHAPTER 2

AN UNTRADITIONAL CHILDHOOD

We were loved and valued . . . exactly as we were.

—GLORIA STEINEM

Gloria Steinem was cherished as a child—and she knew it. That's not to say she didn't have a difficult childhood— her mother, Ruth, suffered from mental illness, and her father, Leo, failed to offer the family financial stability—but Gloria never had reason to question her parents' steadfast love and support. She never doubted that she was loved and that her parents did the best they could. However imperfect, from that secure foundation, Steinem found her place in the world.

Gloria wasn't the first in her family to shatter societal expectations. Her paternal grandmother, Pauline Perlmutter, was a prominent suffragist in Ohio; in 1904, she became the first woman elected to public office in Toledo when she won a seat on the local board of education. In 1914, Perlmutter wrote an essay in the *Toledo Blade* arguing: "I believe in woman suffrage because I believe that the perfect equality of men and women is founded on Divine Wisdom . . . without distinction of race, creed, color or sex." Men and women, she wrote, were "differentiated only by the outer garments, the bodies they temporarily wear." This was a wildly progressive outlook at a time when racism and sexism went unchallenged, and women didn't even have the right to vote.

Joseph Steinem, Gloria's paternal grandfather, was a successful businessman. He was born in Germany and immigrated to the United States to make his fortune as a young man. He saved and invested his money, eventually buying several rental properties and a small brewery in Toledo. After establishing himself financially, he returned to Germany to find a wife. He proposed to Pauline Perlmutter not long after meeting her; she accepted on the condition that he sell the brewery. They married in 1884 and had four sons; their youngest son, Leo, became Gloria's father. Growing up, Leo never had to worry about wealth or status, even during the Great Depression.

Gloria's mother's side of the family had a different relationship with money. Her maternal grandmother, Marie Ochs, was an ambitious, stern, and class-conscious woman who grew up in Dunkirk,

Ohio. She worked outside the home for most of her adult life to supplement the family income, first as a teacher, then a clerk in the office of the recorder of deeds in Dunkirk. Later, she earned extra money by writing sermons for the minister of the Presbyterian church next door.

Marie married Joseph Nuneviller, even though he offered little prospect of upward mobility. Joseph worked as a railroad engineer for the Toledo and Ohio Central. Concerned that he appear professional on his way to work, Marie insisted that he wear a suit on top of his overalls when he left his house in the morning; Joseph slipped off the suit and hung it in his locker when he got to the rail yard. His family remembered that he always ate dessert before his dinner so that he could be sure to have the best part—in case he was called back to work before he finished eating.

Gloria's mother, Ruth Nuneviller, was born in 1898, and her sister, Emma "Janey" Jeanette, was born two years later. Ruth shared her mother's desire for economic security and social status. Gloria remembered her mother telling her about a painful memory of a trip to New York City with Marie when Ruth and Janey were teenagers: "They walked around in the snow, with Marie showing her daughters all the hotels and other things to which they should aspire, but without enough money to go in," Steinem said. "My mother's memory of this was bitter. She felt like a poor person 'with her nose in the glass.'" Too often, both Ruth and her mother focused on what they did not have, instead of what they did.

Marie's parenting style may have triggered some of the anxieties about abandonment that haunted Ruth for the rest of her life. Ruth had been breastfed, but when it was time to wean her, Marie left her infant daughter with a friend and didn't come back until Ruth had learned to drink from a cup. Throughout their childhoods, Marie often left Ruth and her sister alone at home without telling them where she was going or when she would return. Faced with this unpredictability, Ruth learned to worry that the people she loved might disappear or abandon her.

Unlike most women of the time, Marie encouraged her daughters to remain single and secure teaching jobs so that they could support themselves financially. She valued education and encouraged both of her daughters to go to college, which was unusual at the time. In 1916, Ruth enrolled at Oberlin College and Conservatory in Ohio. She took courses in math and history, but writing was her passion. She dreamed of working as a newspaper reporter in New York City.

After two years, money ran tight and Ruth had to transfer to the University of Toledo to complete her education. There she met Leo Steinem, editor of the college newspaper, the *Universi-Teaser*. The two hit it off right away: They both loved puns, poker, and chess. Leo was charming, unpredictable, and adventurous. He made Ruth feel reckless and alive—and the rebellious side of her relished the fact that she knew her mother would never approve of the relationship.

Ruth earned her bachelor's degree in 1920, but she remained at school teaching math and earning a master's degree in American literature. The following year, when Ruth was twenty-three and Leo was twenty-four, the couple went on a picnic. On the way home, Leo spontaneously stopped the car.

"Let's get married," Leo said. "It will only take a minute."

Ruth laughed and impulsively accepted the spur-of-the-moment proposal. They drove to a nearby justice of the peace and got married that afternoon.

Ruth asked Leo to keep the marriage secret. When they went home, they announced their engagement, rather than their marriage. They married a second time a few months later in a ceremony held at Ruth's home. They celebrated their anniversary on October 15, but Leo always gave Ruth two presents, one labeled "To My First Wife" and one labeled "To My Second Wife." In later years, Ruth denied that she and Leo had divorced; she argued that they had been married twice and divorced once, so they were still married.

Both families objected to the relationship. The Nunevillers considered Leo too Jewish, and the Steinems thought Ruth wasn't Jewish enough. Despite the rough start, Ruth felt close to her mother-in-law. Leo's mother was involved with theosophy, a belief system that was popular in the mid- to late-nineteenth century. The religion teaches the unity of living things and the importance of living a moral life. Ruth's acceptance of the religion made her feel more at peace with herself and more accepted by her mother-in-law.

After they married, Ruth taught college calculus for a year. Leo worked odd jobs in a number of fields — journalism, real estate, import-export business, and event promotion. Although they both worked, Ruth and Leo had wildly different attitudes about money. No matter what the bank balance, Leo felt financially secure and Ruth did not. Leo had come from a relatively wealthy family and trusted that his needs would be met; Ruth came from a family that worried about debt and scarcity, and she never believed there was enough.

Early in their marriage, a few of Leo's business investments began to pay off. Using that money—plus some financial assistance from his father—Leo built a house in Toledo. Ruth gave up teaching and took a job writing a gossip column for a small weekly newspaper, *KWK*. She wrote under a male pen name—Duncan MacKenzie—but her work soon earned her offers to write for the *Toledo News-Bee* and the *Toledo Blade* using her own name. She was a good journalist, and she was promoted to editor of the Sunday edition of the *Blade*, which Ruth told Gloria was "the best-paid job on the paper for any employee, male or female." Ruth wanted to be a career journalist, but her life took a different turn when she became pregnant. She became a mother instead of an editor.

When Susanne Steinem was born in 1925, Ruth took a leave from the paper. She initially planned to return to journalism at least part-time, but those plans were dashed when Leo bought property at Clark Lake, Michigan, an isolated rural area about fifty miles northwest of Toledo. Leo decided to develop a resort community with a large entertainment space. He completed the first cottage in 1925. The following year, he built the family home—an impractical Mediterranean-style house with arched openings and an upstairs balcony, which was unheated and not well suited for the cold Michigan winters.

On Memorial Day weekend in 1928, Leo opened Ocean Beach Pier, a dance pavilion at the end of a hundred-foot pier. Colored lights surrounded the black-and-white checkerboard dance floor; advertisements promised dancing "over the water, under the stars." He planned to bring in top musicians and draw weekend crowds from Detroit and Toledo. Gloria said his goal was to create "a resort worthy of the big dance bands of the thirties."

For a brief time, the Steinems prospered. The resort brought in $50,000 the first year it opened—an amount equal to about $735,000 in today's dollars. Susanne attended an elite private school, the family hired a full-time housekeeper, and Ruth shopped at the most expensive stores in Toledo.

But it didn't last.

The first wave of trouble came in the summer of 1929, when Leo added a wooden toboggan run that allowed visitors to ride down and splash into the water. In early July, a seventeen-year-old boy failed to secure the toboggan in place at the top, and he tumbled headfirst into the water, breaking his neck. He died the next day. Ruth became so distraught after the accident that the family physician, Dr. Kenneth Howard, prescribed a sedative that Gloria and her family called "Doc Howard's medicine." Ruth soon became dependent on the medication, which contained chloral hydrate, an addictive sedative.

Several months later, Ruth's father died, leaving her feeling more distraught. And then in the fall of 1929, the stock market crashed, kicking off the Great Depression. The business suffered because people no longer had money for resort vacations. The Steinems could no longer afford to keep their home in Toledo and a second home on Clark Lake, so in 1930 they sold the Toledo house and moved to Clark Lake year-round.

• • • • • • • •

RUTH STRUGGLED WITH feelings of isolation and loneliness. There weren't many neighbors, and she was away from her family in Toledo. In 1930, Ruth became pregnant again. Late in her pregnancy, she started bleeding. She called her mother and asked her to help, but Marie assumed that Ruth was exaggerating about her symptoms. She didn't call the doctor until it was too late. The baby died, and Ruth gave birth to a stillborn son she and Leo named Tom.

To support his family in the off-season, when the resort was closed, Leo began buying and reselling antiques. He traveled for days at a time, leaving Ruth alone at home. Clark Lake was about five miles from the nearest town, and Ruth often felt deserted and frightened when Leo was gone. She began to hear voices in the wind, and on at least one occasion she went five or six days without sleeping. Following that experience, Ruth spent several months in a sanatorium in Toledo.

Family members said she was never the same after the breakdown. Ruth could no longer write or work, and she was not always able to properly parent her children. She became increasingly dependent on Doc Howard's medicine, which helped her sleep.

Despite the family struggles, Susanne begged her parents for a baby sister. Leo thought a new baby might make Ruth happy again. On March 25, 1934, Gloria Marie Steinem was born in Toledo. Ruth and Leo had planned to name her Cynthia, but they decided to let nine-year-old Susanne name her little sister. She chose the name Gloria after her favorite doll. In keeping with Leo's interest in show business, the birth notice announced the "World Premiere Appearance" of Gloria Marie Steinem.

Ruth thrived during the summer of 1934, and Gloria proved to be a beautiful and content baby. But when the days grew shorter and Leo took off for his antiques road tour in the late fall, Ruth began to panic. She felt abandoned and alone. When the radio broke and Ruth could no longer hear the sound of another adult voice, she knew she had to do something before her fears and loneliness overwhelmed her. She didn't have a phone or a car, so when Susanne was at school, Ruth decided to walk five miles into town so that she could talk to another person. She bundled Gloria in warm clothes and began walking, accompanied by the family dog, Fritzie.

As they walked down a hill, a speeding car came over the ridge and hit the dog. Ruth screamed for the driver to stop, but the car kept going. She ran to Fritzie, who was bleeding but still alive. Ruth was determined not to let another car go by, so she sat down in the middle of the road, holding Gloria in one arm and the whimpering dog in the other. Ruth tried to comfort the dog as she waited—half an hour, one hour, two—but no one came. Ruth was alone.

Eventually, the dog quieted. In the late-afternoon darkness of a cold Michigan winter, Fritzie died. Ruth left the dog on the side of the road and walked home to warm up and to wash the blood out of her clothes.

Ruth later told Gloria that she considered the Fritzie experience to be her "breaking point." When Leo returned from his road trip, Ruth told him, "From now on, I'm going with you. I won't bother you. I'll just sit in the car. But I can't be alone again."

Leo honored her wishes. Ruth and the children accompanied Leo on the road, and the family settled into a new normal. In the summers, Gloria swam and explored the lake. She remembered those summers as "a great time of running wild, catching turtles and minnows and setting them free again, looking for coins that customers at my parents' dance hall dropped in the lake, wearing a bathing suit all day long, and sleeping in a little office behind the dance hall."

Susanne and Gloria weren't closely supervised by either Ruth or Leo. Gloria's blond hair was tangled and matted. Every few weeks, her sister would try to comb it out, which was painful and not always successful. For years, Ruth made Gloria wear a red swimsuit so that she could easily spot her daughter at a distance. (When she was eleven years old, Gloria bought herself a black swimsuit and never wore a red one again.) Gloria also spent time with the entertainers in the dance hall. She particularly admired Ruby Brown, who taught Gloria how to tap-dance. For much of her youth, Gloria aspired to be a professional dancer, just like Ruby.

In the late fall and through the winter, the family went on the road. Leo hated cold weather, so he closed up the house, loaded up the car, hooked up a little trailer, and took to the road. Once out of town, they headed for either California or Florida. Along the way, Leo bought and sold antiques, mostly jewelry, china, and knickknacks. The Steinems usually made their way back to Clark Lake by late spring, so that they could freshen up the cottages and be ready to kick off the season on Memorial Day weekend.

The family's financial struggles were real. "My father often had to park the car far away [from the house] to keep it from being repossessed," Steinem said. She remembered sitting in loan offices and pawnshops, trying to come up with enough cash to make ends meet. She learned to recognize the bill collector. By the time she was four years old, she was trained to answer the door and say, "My daddy's not here." Leo was constantly in debt, sometimes mortgaging the house without telling Ruth.

Because of the family's nomadic lifestyle, Gloria missed a great deal of formal education. She often skipped school for months at a time, and some years she didn't go at all. When approached by a truancy officer, Ruth said she homeschooled the children, and she showed her teaching certificate; no one ever looked close enough to notice that she was only qualified to teach college calculus.

While on the road, Gloria and Susanne read everything they could find, including the Nancy Drew stories, the theosophical library, and all the works of Louisa May Alcott. "Louisa May Alcott was my friend," Gloria later recalled. "I read all her adult novels, as well as her young ones, and used to fantasize endlessly that she would come back to life and I could show her all the new things in the world." Gloria identified with the adventurous and independent female characters in Alcott's work; she was also influenced by Alcott's depiction of love and marriage as destructive to women. Gloria particularly loved Jo March from Alcott's novel *Little Women*, who said, "I don't believe I shall ever marry. I'm happy as I am, and love my liberty too well to be in any hurry to give it up for any mortal man."

Despite Gloria's growing skepticism about love and marriage, she forgave her father for his failures and never resented his unpredictable parenting. She didn't consider him irresponsible or delinquent; instead, she thought he was a dreamer, always eager to take advantage of the next big idea. He was an optimist, a risk-taker, an adventurer who believed in the possibilities of tomorrow. He shared his emotions—both joy and sorrow—easily and often. He seemed more alive and engaged in the world than most people. He was fun to be around.

Gloria also appreciated that Leo included her in his jokes and stories. She was part of his team. "He taught me routines," Steinem said. "In crowded elevators, he would turn to me, age five or so, and say, 'So I told the man to keep his fifty thousand dollars.' Or he would say to me, 'If you aren't good you won't go to heaven.' I was supposed to answer, 'I don't want to go to heaven, Daddy, I want to go with you.'" She longed for her father's approval and acceptance, and he willingly gave it to her.

In time, Gloria developed ambivalent feelings about her father. She loved him, but she was embarrassed by him, especially as she got older. Leo weighed more than three hundred pounds, and he couldn't button his jacket. He always looked disheveled and had food stains on his ties. He loved to take Gloria out for ice cream, and he taught her how to get a little bit more from the server when they ordered malted milkshakes. He would send Gloria in to the ice cream store to place her order first, and a few minutes later he would come in and place his own order. By dividing the orders, the person making the shakes would prepare them one at a time, and they could each get the little bit of extra malted milk at the bottom of the mixer. "I loved sitting there at age four or five with my own quarter, pretending not to know my father. He treated me like a grown-up, and I loved him for it," she said.

By example, Leo taught Gloria that she deserved to be treated with love and respect. "He treated me like a friend, asked my advice, enjoyed my company, and thus let me know that I was loved," Gloria wrote in a 1990 essay. "Even in the hardest of times, of which there were many, I knew with a child's unerring sense of fairness that he was treating me as well as he treated himself."

Leo helped shape Gloria's feminist outlook on the world. "Against all he had been taught a man's life should be, against all convention for raising children and especially little girls, he loved and honored me as a unique person," she said. "And that let me know that he and I—and men and women—are not opposites at all."

Even in the dark times, Gloria and her sister knew that they were cherished. Ruth's mental illness did not stop her from loving her daughters. Gloria recalled, "Over and over again, in every way she knew how, she told us that we didn't need to earn her love. We were loved and valued (and therefore we were lovable and valuable) exactly as we were."

· · · · · · · ·

THE FAMILY DYNAMIC changed again when the United States entered World War II in December 1941. People stopped vacationing as money grew tight. The Steinems held on as long as they could, but by 1944, they had to sell the resort.

At that point, the family broke apart: Susanne left home and enrolled at Smith College in Northampton, Massachusetts. Leo turned to the road full-time to try to hustle a living in the antiques world the best way he knew how. Exhausted by years of financial instability and unwilling to continue with life on the road, Ruth asked Leo for a divorce. Ten-year-old Gloria was left alone with her emotionally unstable mother.

RUTH STEINEM

A portrait of Ruth Steinem

[Jess Magoo]

CHAPTER 3

ON
THEIR
OWN

I knew that my mother loved me but that she couldn't take care of me.

— GLORIA STEINEM

G loria Steinem spent the second half of her childhood taking care of her mother. It wasn't supposed to be that way: Ruth Steinem wanted to be the adult and to take care of her daughter, but her fragile mental condition prevented her from being an effective or reliable parent.

For the first few months, it wasn't too bad. Gloria missed her father, but she was relieved that her parents had finally stopped fighting about money. Gloria and Ruth rented a small house in Amherst, Massachusetts, not far from Smith College, where Susanne was a student. In the fall of 1944, when Gloria was in the fifth grade, she attended school regularly for the first time. She looked forward to living a more stable and predictable life.

When she got to school, Gloria realized she was out of step with many of her peers. She had significant gaps in her education: She had been reading independently since she was four years old, but she hadn't been taught much math, history, or science. She didn't know her multiplication facts or how to add and subtract fractions; she was also unaware of how to play common schoolyard games such as jacks or jump rope. She wasn't unintelligent; she was uneducated.

In other ways, Gloria was more mature and worldly than the other fifth graders. She had spent most of her time with adults, so she had developed a more sophisticated sense of humor and vocabulary than most of her classmates. She found herself editing her words and resisting the temptation to make certain jokes so that she could fit in with her new friends. Gloria had learned to read social cues, and she remade herself to meet expectations, making friends and catching up on schoolwork.

At the time, the world was at war—World War II did not end until September 1945—and many adults monitored the news so that their children would not become frightened. Rather than shielding Gloria from too much information about the war, Ruth shared all the details she learned, telling her about the Nazis, anti-Semitism, and, when they were discovered, the specifics of what went on inside the concentration camps. Insecurity and instability rocked the world; Gloria didn't have much to hold on to to feel safe.

Gloria missed her father. He came to visit once that winter, arriving on a snowy afternoon. Gloria went sledding with friends, and when she came back, Ruth and Leo had made hot chocolate. What was common for so many children became a formative memory for Gloria: a perfect snow day, when she could feel like she was part of a happy, traditional family. But Leo didn't stay. After a brief visit, he went back on the road, selling antiques and working his way back to his new home in California.

Leo wrote letters to Gloria, but they saw each other only once or twice a year. "Between visits he sent postcards signed 'Pop,'" Gloria said. He also sent fifty-dollar money orders enclosed in stationery embossed not with his name and address but exploding red letters: "It's Steinemite!"

During the school year, Ruth's condition stabilized. That summer, Susanne took a job in New York City and Gloria and her mother followed, moving to the house of one of Ruth's college friends in Scarsdale, New York, a suburb just north of the city. It was a lonely summer: Ruth didn't have a car, they didn't know anyone, and the damp, dark house where they were staying felt uncomfortable and unwelcoming. As the weeks passed, Ruth slipped into a deep depression and began hallucinating. Once again, she began to rely on Doc Howard's medicine to calm her nerves, with mixed results. Throughout the summer, Gloria stayed at home with her mother, reading and, when necessary, reassuring Ruth that they were safe and no one meant them harm.

In the fall, Gloria and her mother moved back to Toledo. They had planned to live in the farmhouse on Woodville Road where Ruth had grown up, which had been divided into three rental apartments. Since Ruth had moved away, the neighborhood had suffered from neglect. A four-lane highway had been built right next to the house, and many of the surrounding buildings had been abandoned or torn down.

When they arrived, all three apartments were rented, so Ruth and Gloria moved to a basement apartment in a rooming house on the other side of town. Their apartment consisted of a space behind the furnace room, with a tiny kitchen and bathroom beyond. Gloria and her mother slept in bunk beds because the crowded room wasn't large enough to fit two twin beds side by side. The small windows looked out at the tires of the cars parked in the driveway.

In the late 1940s, Toledo was an industrial city, home of several major factories. When the wind blew the wrong way, the fumes from the smokestacks soured the air across East Toledo. In this working-class neighborhood, sex roles were clearly defined: Women became wives and mothers; men worked in the factories, drove trucks, or held white-collar jobs selling insurance or running small businesses.

Gloria didn't see her future in Toledo. Not unlike her father or the characters in Louisa May Alcott's novels, she wanted a life of independence and adventure. She didn't know what tomorrow promised, but she did know that she didn't want to be trapped in working-class Toledo for the rest of her life.

In these years, Gloria became very aware of class. "Class was very important to me and what I became," Steinem later wrote. "Neighborhood women were clearly divided into victims and nice girls, and if you became a victim, not a nice girl, your life was over." She vowed that she would never allow herself to become a victim.

Gloria enrolled in the sixth grade at nearby Monroe Elementary School. She delighted in learning that she was nearsighted so that she should get glasses, which made her feel grown-up. Her glasses and long straight hair became a key part of her unique style later in life.

During this time, Gloria developed an elaborate fantasy life, often imagining a day when she would discover that Ruth and Leo were not her actual parents. "Though I loved my parents and knew I wasn't adopted, I used to fantasize endlessly that my real parents would come get me and take me to a neat house with a room of my own, and a horse in a field next door," Steinem wrote. She also had rescue fantasies, but hers weren't typical: Instead of dreaming that someone else rushed in to rescue her, Gloria imagined that she was the one who controlled the scene and saved someone else. In one of these heroine dreams, she envisioned that she pushed into a crowd to save a man who was about to be lynched. Gloria may not have felt powerful in her daily life, but she was empowered in her fantasy life.

• • • • • • • •

ALTHOUGH SHE DID her best, Ruth couldn't appropriately care for Gloria. "I knew that my mother loved me, but that she couldn't take care of me," Gloria said. Instead, the mother/daughter roles were reversed: Gloria took care of her mother, making her bologna sandwiches at mealtimes and comforting her when she had nightmares.

Ruth was a very sick woman. "For many years, I . . . never

imaged my mother any way other than . . . someone to be worried about and cared for; an invalid who lay in bed with eyes closed and lips moving in occasional response to voices only she could hear." Ruth remained addicted to Doc Howard's medicine. Most of the time it calmed her nerves, but sometimes it seemed to contribute to Ruth's hallucinations.

The following year, one of the tenants moved out so Gloria and her mother could move to the upstairs apartment in the run-down farmhouse where Ruth had grown up. One of the downstairs apartments was rented by a local butcher and his family; the third unit was occupied by a noisy man who beat his pregnant wife.

The apartment at the farmhouse was more spacious than the furnace room, but it left much to be desired. Ruth and Gloria's apartment didn't have a kitchen sink. They let the dirty dishes pile up day after day, eventually washing them in the bathtub when they needed clean plates and cutlery.

Rats infested the house. The sound of rodents scurrying around and scratching inside the walls often kept Gloria up at night. Once a rat bit Gloria badly enough that her mother had to take her to the emergency room for treatment. One of the neighbors complained that the rats were so large and aggressive that they had killed three kittens in the downstairs apartment. Ruth didn't know how to handle the problem, so Gloria became proficient at setting rat traps.

Gloria never knew what to expect when she came home from school. Some days Ruth was so quiet that no one knew she was home; other times she could be loud and frantic, violently fighting off the demons that possessed her. "I remember so well the dread of not knowing who I would find when I came home," Gloria recalled years later. "A mother whose speech was slurred by tranquilizers, a woman wandering in the neighborhood not sure of where she was, or a loving and sane woman who asked me about my school day. I created a cheerful front and took refuge in constant reading and after-school jobs—anything to divert myself (and others) from the realities of my life."

On most days, Gloria's mother had little hold on reality. One day she worried that German troops had invaded their street and were coming for them; another time Ruth was convinced that Gloria's sister had been killed in a traffic accident. On more than one occasion, Ruth forgot that Gloria had an after-school job and called the police to report her daughter missing. When Gloria came home from school, she sometimes found her mother wandering in her nightgown on the street, calling for her. Once, she came home to find her mother painting the windows black. Another time, Gloria found Ruth tossing clothes out the window.

It wasn't often, but sometimes Gloria became frustrated with her mother. "Humiliated in front of my friends . . . I would yell at her—and she would bow her head in fear and say, 'I'm sorry, I'm sorry, I'm sorry,' just as she had done so often when my otherwise-kindhearted father had yelled at her in frustration," Steinem later wrote. "Perhaps the worst thing about suffering is that it finally hardens the hearts of those around it."

At one point, Ruth's hallucinations reached the point that Gloria went for help from the doctor who had run the Toledo sanatorium where Ruth had stayed years before. After a brief interview, the doctor told Gloria that her mother should be committed to the state hospital. Gloria hesitated. She had read articles about state mental asylums in *Life* magazine, and she refused to send her mother to such a heartless place. She left and vowed to continue to take care of her mother on her own.

Gloria knew that other adults—specifically her father and her aunt Janey—knew about her mother's situation and didn't do anything to help, so they must have considered it acceptable. When she tried to discuss her concerns with her father, Leo pushed back. "How can I travel and take care of your mother?" he asked. "How can I make a living?"

Gloria didn't see any alternatives or solutions. She accepted that her father would remain somewhat involved in her life, although it was on his terms. He sent oranges from Florida and packages at birthdays and Christmas. He showed up unannounced once or twice a year, typically driving a late-model Cadillac, which he lived out of most of the time. These visits lifted Gloria's spirits, but they never lasted long. Rather than blame her parents for their failings, she accepted that they were both doing the best they could to take care of her.

Recognizing that her emotional needs could not be met by her family, Gloria looked outside of her family for affirmation. "At home it felt dangerous," she said. "I felt safer outside." Gloria became a joiner. In junior high, she joined a Girl Scouts troop and worked tirelessly to earn merit badges. When she was old enough to earn a paycheck, she took on part-time jobs. She played records at the local radio station, sold clothes at a retail store, and appeared as a magician's assistant. She joined a dance troupe known as the Christian Convalescent Entertainment Society and performed routines at nursing homes, the Eagles club, and supermarket openings. She also danced with the Toledo Symphony Orchestra, earning ten dollars per show.

In high school, Gloria and the popular girls in her class formed a sorority. She dated a boy several years older; he was good-looking, he loved to dance, and he drove a Ford convertible. She auditioned for Ted Mack's *Original Amateur Hour*, hoping to win a spot on the show and tap-dance her way out of Toledo. (She wasn't chosen.) She also entered a local beauty and talent contest, again hoping to find a way to get out of town. (She didn't win; she was first runner-up.)

Years later, Gloria hesitated to speak openly about her childhood. When she did share some of the details, people who disagreed with her politics charged her with exaggerating the hardships of her past. In defense of Gloria, a woman who lived in the downstairs apartment wrote to the *Blade* in 1972 to verify Steinem's account, specifically the description of the rat infestation. The former neighbor disavowed Steinem's position on feminism, but she confirmed her description of the Toledo house. "The house was in a bad state of disrepair and very definitely overrun with rats," wrote Lillian Barnes Borton. "The rats would even get up on our beds at night, they were in our kitchen range and sink cabinet . . . I remember when Gloria was bitten by the rats. Mrs. Steinem was so terribly upset that she cried."

While Gloria and her mother were still living in the apartment, the town condemned the house. The heat was shut off because the furnace wasn't in good repair, so Gloria and her mother huddled together in the same bed on cold nights. It came as a relief when the Presbyterian church next door offered to buy the house and lot for $8,000, an amount equal to about $78,000 in today's dollars. Gloria was a junior in high school, and Ruth worried about finding the money to send her to college. After some consideration, Ruth decided to sell the house and set aside the money for Gloria's college education. That left one problem: They needed somewhere to live while Gloria finished high school.

Washington, DC, where Gloria's sister,
Susanne, lived and worked
[Library of Congress]

CHAPTER 4

SENIOR YEAR

One year is all. We're synchronizing our watches.

— LEO STEINEM

In the summer of 1951, the Steinem family gathered in Toledo to figure out where Gloria and Ruth should live once the boarding house was sold. Gloria had one more year of high school, and she needed to attend a school that would help her prepare for college.

Gloria's sister, Susanne, had an idea: She worked in Washington, DC, and offered to have Gloria live with her during her senior year. Susanne could not take care of her mother as well, so for her plan to work Leo would have to agree to take responsibility for his ex-wife.

The family met for breakfast at a small restaurant in town. Susanne presented the proposal to Leo, who refused to consider it. "No, we're divorced," Leo said. "And besides, I can't work if I'm taking care of her." Someone needed to take care of Ruth, and he didn't consider her his burden anymore.

Susanne tried to persuade her father to change his mind for Gloria's sake. It wasn't fair. Gloria deserved to have at least one year of high school without feeling obligated to take care of her mother.

Leo wouldn't budge. His answer was no.

Susanne stormed out of the restaurant, leaving Leo to drive Gloria to her job at a local boutique. Always stoic, Gloria climbed into her father's car and looked out the window. Overcome with despair, she began to weep. She had allowed herself to imagine a different life, a normal life. She had dared to hope for happiness, but once again, no one seemed to be concerned with what she needed.

Gloria's pain surprised her father. He had not seen her cry since she was a tiny child. Leo loved his daughter, and he saw how much this chance at freedom meant to her. Against his wishes, he changed his mind and agreed to take Ruth with him to California for one year.

"All right," Leo said. "But one year is all. We're synchronizing our watches."

. . . .

GLORIA AND HER sister had a strong relationship. When they were growing up, if they had a disagreement, their mother would insist that both sisters make peace and say, "We are sisters and have to love each other." Ruth felt compelled to build a bond between her daughters because she felt that her mother had undermined her relationship with her own sister. In Ruth's childhood, her mother had fostered competition and distrust between Ruth and her sister, Janey, by comparing the two and praising one in opposition to the other. In an attempt to learn from her mother's mistakes, Ruth encouraged family unity and sisterly love.

With that closeness at the core, Gloria moved to Washington, DC, and enrolled at Western High School. Living with twenty-six-year-old Susanne was nothing like living with Ruth: Susanne worked as a gemologist and had her own local television show, *Gem Session*. The sisters shared a town house in Georgetown with two other roommates, both single career women. Initially, Susanne's roommates weren't eager to share their apartment with a high school senior, but Gloria won them over. In the weeks before school started, Gloria spent time at a nearby hotel that charged nonresidents a dollar to use the pool. A junior naval officer met Gloria and asked her out on a date; when she brought the officer home, the roommates were impressed that she had attracted a man that they would have been interested in. From that point forward, they no longer treated her like an unwelcome little sister. Gloria's good looks and ability to attract men gave her status in the eyes of her sister's friends.

At first, Gloria was anxious about enrolling at a new school. She knew how to reinvent herself and start over—this was her sixth new school—but Western High was more academically and socially elite than the schools she was used to. These were the children of diplomats and congressmembers, not truck drivers and factory workers. Almost all the students at Western planned to attend college, rather than marry and start a family, which was the shared fate of most of the girls in Toledo.

With fake-it-till-you-make-it confidence, Gloria took Western High by storm. She joined a high school sorority, attended dances, and earned a part in the spring play. She was elected vice president of the student council, vice president of the senior class (only boys could be president), secretary of the French club, and a staff member of the school yearbook. She was voted Prettiest Girl in the senior class. While Gloria hesitated to attribute her achievements to her beauty, her appearance undoubtedly made it easier for her to attain social acceptance and status. She enjoyed the approval of her classmates, but most of all, Gloria enjoyed the freedom of not feeling responsible for her mother.

Although she embraced student life, Gloria refused to be frivolous and self-centered. Unlike her classmates who spent hours talking about boys and college, Gloria liked to discuss social issues, such as poverty and civil rights. She seemed older and more sophisticated than most of her peers. She learned to wear makeup and painted her long fingernails bright colors. She didn't talk much about her parents, and most of her peers assumed they weren't around because they were in the foreign service and assigned to an overseas post.

Despite her poised exterior, Gloria lived in fear of revealing her inadequacies. She worked double-time to make up for her academic weaknesses, and she did her best to hide or fill in other gaps in her upbringing. For example, she dated the school heartthrob and was mortified when she had to tell him that she didn't know the difference between a lobster and a crab. She had never eaten either one.

With the backing of her family, Gloria had every intention of going to college. Her grades weren't fantastic, and her college board scores were weak, but her high school guidance counselor took an interest in her and wrote a strong letter of recommendation. Gloria applied to Cornell and Stanford—both rejected her—but her first choice was Smith College, the all-women's school that her sister had attended. She was accepted at Smith. Her mother had set aside money from the sale of the house to finance Gloria's education, so money was not an obstacle.

For years, the Steinems had hoped that Ruth's condition could be managed or controlled without outside support. By the time Gloria graduated from high school, Susanne had accepted that her mother was seriously ill and needed ongoing care. She identified a psychiatric hospital in Baltimore that provided treatment with the goal of having patients return to their communities at some point. Again, Susanne persuaded the family that long-term psychiatric treatment was Ruth's best chance for ongoing health and stability.

On June 12, 1952, Gloria graduated from Western High School. Neither Ruth nor Leo attended the ceremony, which allowed Gloria to enjoy the day without distraction or embarrassment. With Ruth in residence at a safe and caring facility and Leo happy on the road, Gloria was able to attend Smith and focus on her future.

Smith College

[The Miriam and Ira D. Wallach Division of Art, Prints and Photographs:
Photography Collection, The New York Public Library]

CHAPTER 5

SMITH

Don't worry about your background. Whether it's odd or ordinary, use it, build on it.

— GLORIA STEINEM

During the summer of 1952, the summer after her high school graduation, Gloria Steinem met several young women from Smith while volunteering with Adlai Stevenson's presidential campaign. Gloria—typically poised, confident, and self-assured—withered in their presence. Intimidated by their worldliness, she began to question herself. Would she fit in at Smith, which was at the peak of its reputation as the college of choice for privileged and prominent young women? She felt like an impostor: Would the other students see through her act and realize she was a fraud?

When she explained her feelings to Susanne, her sister tried to reassure Gloria, explaining that not all Smith coeds were well-to-do. Many came from affluent backgrounds—and, admittedly, some came from *very* affluent families—but Gloria would find her way once she got to campus. Susanne didn't tell her little sister at the time, but she understood Gloria's insecurities. She didn't mention that some of the girls arrived on campus in limousines. And she didn't share the story of how she was taken aback when she met her roommate freshman year and the girl smiled approvingly and said that she was relieved to meet her because "with a name like Steinem we were afraid you might be a Jew."

In addition to fretting about how she would be accepted, Gloria worried about how her mother would handle the adjustment to life with Susanne in Washington, DC. Leo had promptly returned to California after dropping Ruth with Susanne, and no one knew how the transition was going to go. Gloria knew that Susanne was a competent adult in her late twenties, but she also knew that she had more experience than anyone else with navigating her mother's mood swings. Gloria knew better than Susanne how difficult her mother could be on her darkest days.

Gloria's fears were realized on the day she left for Smith. Gloria and Susanne accidentally missed their train to Northampton, Massachusetts, so they returned to their apartment to wait for the next train. When they got home, they discovered that Ruth had taken an overdose of Doc Howard's medicine, and she was losing consciousness. Susanne was terrified because she had never seen her mother in this condition; Gloria was terrified because she had, and she knew her mother's condition remained fragile. Unsure of what to do, they monitored Ruth's condition, settled her into bed, and left on a later afternoon train.

After she arrived on campus, it did not take long for Gloria to fall into the rhythm of college life. She thought about her mother often and checked with her by phone, but Gloria didn't want Ruth to be her responsibility. For the first time in her life, Gloria was able to focus on her schoolwork without distraction. She relaxed, knowing she had a safe and clean place to live and she had access to healthy meals on a regular schedule. Her classmates took the college lifestyle for granted, but Gloria delighted in the comfort of having a stable living arrangement for the next four years.

At first, Gloria struggled academically. Her grades weren't strong, especially in French and science, but her writing helped bring up her average. By her sophomore year, she figured out how to study and apply herself, and she was on the dean's list for the rest of her time in college. (She was admitted to the honor society Phi Beta Kappa because it didn't count freshman-year grades when choosing students.) She developed an interest in international politics and decided to major in government.

While Gloria did not enjoy science courses, she said that her freshman geology class proved to be one of the most valuable courses she took at Smith, although not because of what she learned in class. "I took geology because I thought it was the least scientific of the sciences," Steinem wrote. On a class trip to the

Connecticut River, she became distracted by a large turtle that was crawling along the side of the road. Steinem worried that it was going to be hit by a car, so she carried it back to the river.

When she was finished, her geology professor told her, "You know, that turtle probably spent a month crawling up to the dirt road to lay its eggs in the mud by the side of the road, and you just put it back in the river."

Steinem felt terrible. Years later, she remembered the incident but saw it as a political lesson, a caution about authoritarian impulses on both the left and right. She knew she should not impose her vision of what was right for someone else. However well-intentioned she might be, she should always ask the people what they need and want because she may not really understand their point of view. "Always ask the turtle," she said.

Political-science classes appealed to Gloria, and she had no trouble grasping the concepts. Her classmates considered her very bright and engaged. She enjoyed late-night discussions, where she proved herself to be both a good listener and a good conversationalist. Too often she procrastinated with assignments, often writing papers at the last minute. During her sophomore year, a professor told her that she wrote easily and well.

"What do you mean 'easily'?" Gloria replied.

"If you're so paranoid that you notice the word *easily* and not the word *well*, that just shows you're a real writer," he said.

Both academically and socially, Gloria continued to feel like an impostor. She always saw herself as a little bit different from her classmates. Gloria had her own style. While most Smith coeds dressed the same—Bermuda shorts, knee socks, blouses with cardigans, and pearl necklaces—Gloria wore heavy eye makeup, glitzy costume jewelry, and jeans with sweatshirts. She kept her nails long and polished, a habit she had developed in Toledo. Gloria learned to barter her skills with those of her classmates: She taught her friends how to apply makeup or iron a dress, in exchange for tutoring in French or help with math assignments. "Don't worry about your background," she said, "whether it's odd or ordinary, use it, build on it."

Gloria had learned from her father how to tell funny stories, and she entertained her friends with tales about life in Toledo and Clark Lake. She kept the anecdotes light and amusing, never revealing the pain and insecurity she sometimes felt. She talked about the winters on the road, traveling cross-country in a house trailer. She joked that one year they left Clark Lake in such a hurry that they left the dirty dishes in the sink. "We've just finished washing last year's dishes" was the punch line, always good for a laugh. She made her childhood sound fun in a lighthearted, wacky way, rather than unsettling in a frightening, mentally ill way.

At Smith, Gloria never told the truth about her mother's mental illness or the poverty and challenges of her life in Toledo. These topics were too private—and too painful—to share. The truth was that Ruth continued to struggle after Gloria left for college. Susanne wrote to Gloria and explained in great detail what was being done about their mother's mental health. Susanne had taken Ruth to several doctors, all of whom agreed that she needed to be institutionalized, at least temporarily, for a condition diagnosed as chronic anxiety neurosis. Susanne refused to commit her—she thought that would be too frightening for her mother—so she tried to convince her to surrender voluntarily.

Susanne explored Saint Elizabeths, a government-operated mental institution near Washington, DC, but she worried about how Ruth might be treated. She looked at other facilities and finally decided on Sheppard and Enoch Pratt Hospital, a private facility in Baltimore. To pay for treatment, they sold some of their mother's property at Clark Lake, which Ruth had acquired as part of the divorce settlement. Ruth remained at the Baltimore facility for several months, first in a locked ward and then moving to a less-controlled program.

The summer after her freshman year, Gloria stayed with Susanne in Washington, DC, and visited her mother in Baltimore every weekend. In time, Ruth was able to take trips away from the hospital with her daughters. During this period of her life, Gloria began to see her mother as her own person, separate from her, no longer simply the demanding and ill person who had depended so completely on her young daughter. Gloria finally appreciated that she and her mother were two distinct women, each with her own path forward.

As her mental health improved over several years, Ruth moved from the hospital to a Quaker halfway house to an apartment in a rooming house in Washington, DC. While Ruth went in and out of care over the years, Gloria was never again the primary caretaker for her mother. The part of her life where she was defined as her mother's keeper had ended.

• • • • • • • •

GLORIA APPLIED TO study in Europe during her junior year at Smith. In the fall of 1954, she and about fifty other Smith coeds spent six weeks in Paris taking French classes before traveling to the University of Geneva in Switzerland to study history, law, and literature. At the time, Gloria could not imagine that she would ever have another chance to see Europe. After such an exciting adventure, she didn't want to return home, so she applied for—and won—a scholarship to study literature and political science at Oxford University in England for the summer.

When she returned to Smith for her senior year, Gloria thought she might want to study law after graduation. She spoke to a guidance counselor who asked: "Why study three extra years and end up in the back room of some law firm doing research and typing, when you can graduate from Smith and do research and typing right away?"

Gloria didn't pursue the law. Instead, her life took a different turn that fall when she fell in love with Blair Chotzinoff and became engaged to be married. Gloria wasn't comfortable marrying him—but she wasn't ready to end the relationship, either. They had a strong physical and emotional connection, and she felt unsure of what to do.

On June 3, 1956, Gloria graduated magna cum laude—with great honor—from Smith College. She had started out struggling with her grades, but she finished as one of the top students in her class. Her father, mother, and sister attended the ceremony and watched Gloria receive her diploma. Following graduation, Gloria went to Washington, DC, to stay with her mother and finish planning her upcoming wedding. She struggled with the decision but finally decided to break off the engagement. She loved her fiancé, but she knew marriage would be the wrong path for her at that time.

When she was seeing Chotzinoff, Gloria had convinced a

doctor to provide her with a diaphragm for birth control. She worried that her mother might discover her contraception and find out she was sexually active, so she threw it away after she ended the relationship. But things weren't that simple. Gloria went to New York to see Chotzinoff one last time, and they ended up sleeping together. The passion they shared made the decision to end the relationship more difficult, but she knew the marriage would be a mistake.

Gloria worried that the sexual attraction between them would be too great and that she would end up changing her mind and becoming unhappily married. To avoid the temptation of being near her former fiancé, she applied for a one-year postgraduate fellowship to study in India as a Chester Bowles scholar through a Smith international relations organization. She had learned through a friend that one of the scholarship recipients had been unable to accept, so she wrote to the program director and explained that she was no longer engaged and welcomed the opportunity to study abroad. The committee awarded her the fellowship, and in early December she flew to London to wait for her visa to India.

London, circa 1950
[Nasjonalbiblioteket]

CHAPTER 6

ABORTION

I couldn't admit that I was the one who didn't want to get married.

—GLORIA STEINEM

Gloria Steinem arrived in London in early December to wait for her visa to India to come through. During this time, she lived with the family of a friend from college and worked as a waitress at an espresso bar to make a little extra money. She had assumed the paperwork would come through in a couple of weeks, but the process took longer than expected.

Several weeks after she arrived in England, Steinem began to suspect that she might be pregnant. Her period was late, and she and Blair hadn't used birth control the last time they had sex.

She didn't know what to do.

Without telling a soul, she went to the library to try to find advice on how to end a pregnancy. Ideas like throwing herself down the stairs or douching with dangerous chemicals didn't sound safe—or effective. It soon became clear that she couldn't abort the baby by herself. She didn't want to get married, and she didn't want to have a child, whether she kept it or put it up for adoption. She had seen too many girls in Toledo forced into marriage and motherhood too soon, and she had witnessed the shame and stigma placed on unwed mothers. At age twenty-three, Steinem wasn't ready to surrender her freedom and independence: After spending most of her childhood taking care of her mother, she didn't want to be responsible for someone else again.

Steinem didn't trust anyone with her secret. She didn't tell her former fiancé, the father of the baby, Blair Chotzinoff. She didn't tell her sister or her mother. She didn't tell her friend from Smith, the only person she knew in London. She knew she would have to solve the issue on her own. She had heard about abortions, but all she knew was that "you didn't *necessarily* die" from them. And abortions were illegal.

Steinem—alone, frightened, trapped—considered suicide.

But she didn't want to die. She simply wanted to end her pregnancy.

She looked in the phone book and found a doctor located near the apartment where she was staying. She made an appointment with Dr. John E. Sharpe, and when she saw him several days later she said that she was worried she might be pregnant. She told him that she was a jilted lover, a woman abandoned by a man who refused to marry her, even though she thought she was pregnant. "I told him a long story about how this man didn't want to marry me," she said. "Because I thought I couldn't admit that I was the one who didn't want to get married."

To confirm the pregnancy, the doctor wrote her a prescription for a medication that would induce her period if she were not pregnant. The medicine did not work, confirming her worst fears.

During this time, Steinem tried to continue with her life as usual. While attending a party she happened to have a passing conversation with a loud and egocentric American playwright who complained that he had to coordinate abortions for two actresses in his play who were pregnant. Trying to keep the conversation casual, Steinem asked if he had to send them to France for the procedure. He explained that abortions were legal in England if two doctors agreed that the procedure was medically necessary.

The following day, Steinem returned to Dr. Sharpe's office. She pleaded with him to help her get an abortion, and he cautiously agreed to be one of the two required signatures. Abortion was legal, but doctors agreed to it reluctantly. The doctor gave Steinem two conditions: She should not tell anyone that he had authorized the procedure (and she didn't reveal his name until years after his death), and second, that "she promise to do what she really wanted with her life." He handed Steinem the necessary paperwork and gave her the name of a female surgeon who could provide the second signature and perform the procedure.

Steinem immediately went to the second doctor, who she found to be condescending and unsympathetic but still willing to perform the abortion. The doctor was competent; the procedure was safe; the abortion was legal. Steinem knew she was one of the lucky ones: Abortion was not legal in the United States and women regularly suffered—and often died—while trying to end their pregnancies.

After the abortion, Steinem stayed in bed for a few days. She told her roommate that her back hurt. She then returned to work, relieved and grateful that the experience was behind her. The abortion had cost almost half the thousand dollars she had brought with her to spend in India, but the money wasn't as important as the freedom it provided.

Years later, when Steinem reflected on her abortion, she noted that it was "the first time I stopped passively accepting whatever happened to me and took responsibility." However harrowing the experience had been, Steinem emerged with a greater sense of control over her own decisions. She wanted to take charge of her life and make choices for herself, accepting full responsibility for the consequences.

For a time, Steinem felt isolated and depressed, but she was determined to go on with her life. "My own [abortion] had taken place in a time of such isolation, illegality, and fear that afterward, I did my best to just forget," Steinem later wrote. With the experience behind her, she did her best to move forward. When her visa came through, she set out for India.

Bombay, now called Mumbai, India, 1957

[Alamy]

CHAPTER 7

INDIA

Most of us have a few events that divide our lives into "before" and "after." This was one for me.

— GLORIA STEINEM

On February 4, 1957, Gloria Steinem arrived in Bombay, India, a city now called Mumbai. From there she traveled on to Delhi, where she enrolled in an academic program at the University of Delhi as part of her fellowship program.

From the moment she arrived, Steinem experienced a freedom to be herself. Throughout her life she had felt like an outsider, always struggling to read the social cues to figure out how to behave and fit in; in India, she was so undeniably different that she couldn't pass as a local. Rather than struggling to meet anyone's expectations, she opened herself up to the newness of being in a different country and culture. Instead of trying to interpret the experience by looking through the lens of a camera or recording her observations with a notebook and pen, Steinem simply surrendered to the moment and embraced being a young woman on her own in India.

Steinem felt oddly at home. No one knew what to make of her, so she didn't have to define herself through other people's expectations. As long as she dressed in appropriately modest female clothing, she was free to be herself and explore the country and its people.

Steinem darkened her hair, wore kohl around her eyes, and learned to wear a sari. She learned how to eat with her hands from plantain-leaf plates, how to bow with praying hands in greeting, and how to accept—and respectfully decline—the many invitations she received to share coffee and meals. She did her best to answer questions asked by the Indian students, who wanted to know about Western culture.

Every few months, Steinem reported what she was learning to the scholarship committee at Smith. In addition to sharing what she learned about Indian culture, she told them that she answered questions about Western culture, including topics such as Christianity, lingerie, the dating system, rock and roll, how much milk the average American cow gives, favorite authors, and the politics of arming Pakistan against India.

Steinem also wrote to the scholarship committee about the extreme poverty she witnessed. Early in her stay, while she was adjusting to life in India, she wrote: "How will I ever, *ever* become accustomed to the bundle of dirty rags on the sidewalk which often as not turns out to be a little boy . . . or the leper who stretches out his fingerless hands to beg; or the sweeper-woman who trails a wandering cow that she may catch its dung and form it into patties of fuel."

In her coursework at the university, Steinem learned more about the recent history of India. At the time of her stay, the country had been independent from colonial rule for only about ten years. In 1947, India became independent from the British after Mohandas Gandhi led the nation in a thirty-year struggle to achieve self-rule through nonviolent revolution. (Gandhi's model of peaceful protest became the model for the civil rights activism of Martin Luther King Jr. in the United States.) Unfortunately, Gandhi was assassinated in 1948, and the young country fell into a bloody religious war that left the country divided into predominantly Hindu India and predominantly Muslim Pakistan.

Steinem admired and respected Gandhi's teachings. In a previous academic class, she had written a paper about the Communist Party in India, noting that the Communists had objected to the independence movement and supported British colonialism. Steinem steadfastly supported Gandhian principles because his approach was both nonviolent and democratic. Up to that point, her understanding of Gandhian principles had been theoretical and academic; when the chance arose, she was eager to put those ideas into practice.

• • • • • • • •

AFTER THREE MONTHS of study, the Smith scholarship program ended, but Steinem didn't want to go home. Instead, she decided to stay in India and travel on her own. She spent about a month in Calcutta, then went south to Madras (now Chennai), traveling in third class on the railroad to save money. She journeyed alone, and she sometimes went weeks at a time without seeing another Westerner.

Steinem was appalled by the Indian caste system, which divided people into social classes at birth. A person's caste strictly determined access to education and work opportunities. Mahatma Gandhi had worked to destroy the caste system so that people could "be respected as one, all religions as one." Gandhi had been a revolutionary. "He literally turned the hierarchy on its head, not by giving orders but by himself making the bottom rung his standard of living," Steinem said. "He led by example."

In Madras, Steinem met up with a group of Gandhians, people who continued the work of Mahatma Gandhi by trying to end the caste riots that were taking place in Southern India. Villages were being burned and people were being killed in violent outbreaks that were encouraged by local politicians who thought they could use the conflict to their political advantage. The Gandhians walked from village to village, holding meetings to encourage people to respond to the hostilities with nonviolence.

Steinem joined the Gandhians on their quest. They needed women to assist with the effort because only a woman could enter the female quarters and invite the women in the village to attend the meetings. In addition, a woman could attend a public meeting only if another woman was present. Steinem was the only woman on the mission at that time, so her participation was essential. She supported the mission, so she left her pack behind and joined the operation, traveling with only a towel, a cup, and a comb.

The experience had a profound impact on Gloria's life. "I found there was a freedom in having no possessions . . . a peacefulness in focusing only on the moment at hand. I remember this as the first time in my life when I was living completely in the present."

The teams typically walked from five to eleven in the morning, rested during the midday heat, and walked on, sometimes hiking for as much as thirteen hours a day. When they arrived at a village that had been burned, they reached out to the people, giving them a voice and a chance to talk about what had happened. They listened and encouraged people to choose the path of peace and nonviolence rather than revenge.

"Each day, we set off along paths shaded by palms and sheltered by banyan trees, cut across plowed fields, and waded into streams to cool off and let our homespun clothes dry on us as we walked," Steinem wrote. "In the villages, families shared their food and sleeping mats with us, women taught me how to wash my sari and wash and oil my hair."

She also learned a lot by listening. "There were so many stories of atrocities and vengeance . . . that it was hard to imagine how it could end," she wrote. "But gradually, people expressed relief at having been listened to, at seeing neighbors who had been too afraid to come out of their houses, and at hearing facts brought by [the Gandhian] team, for the rumors were even more terrible than the events themselves. To my amazement . . . meetings often ended with village leaders pledging to take no revenge on caste groups whose members had attacked their group in a neighboring village." Steinem found that listening to the people was one of the most important instruments of change.

Steinem learned about talking circles and the power of allowing people to tell their own stories. Stories are the heartbeat of all social justice movements. "Every great social justice movement has started with consciousness, and that means, in a practical sense, people sitting around, in a circle, telling their personal stories," Steinem said. People move from thinking that their experience is unique to realizing that other people have had similar challenges. At some point, people usually realize that something that happens to a lot of people is political, not personal. That is the spark that can ignite social change: People realize, Steinem argued, that "if we get together, we can do something about it."

Her experience listening to people in India also taught Steinem a lot about organizing. She learned several key principles from Gandhi's followers: "If you do something the people care about, the people will take care of you. If you want people to listen to you, you have to listen to them. If you hope people will change how they live, you have to know how they live. If you want people to see you, you have to sit down with them eye to eye."

These experiences changed the direction of Steinem's life. She learned about herself and about building social change from the ground up. "Most of us have a few events that divide our lives into 'before' and 'after,'" Steinem said. "This was one for me."

• • • • • • • •

IN THE END, it wasn't a change of heart but the need for a change of socks that ended Steinem's time in Southern India. She had developed serious blisters from all the walking, and some had become deep, infected sores. When she finally consulted a doctor, he gave her penicillin and told her she had to stop marching. She made her way back to Bombay, where she explored the city and tried to earn enough money to return to the United States. She wasn't in a hurry; she remained in Bombay for almost a year.

Steinem used her status as an attractive, white American to support herself while she was in India. She was hired by an ad agency to write an article from a Western tourist's perspective. She also posed in ads for toothpaste, shampoo, and cold cream. She worked for a company interested in exporting sandals, both designing sandals and writing promotional material for them. Finally, she got a three-month assignment that would pay enough to finance her travel home: The Indian Tourist Bureau hired her to write *The Thousand Indias*, a travel guidebook that would entice Westerners to visit India and explore beyond the key attractions of Delhi, the Taj Mahal, and Jaipur.

In July 1958, Steinem sailed toward California in steerage on an ocean liner named the *President Cleveland*. She traveled with several hundred Chinese immigrants and a fundamentalist Christian family.

When Steinem arrived in the United States, Leo met her in San Francisco. He didn't have enough money for gas to make it all the way back east, so they headed for Las Vegas because Leo thought Gloria was lucky. "In a windowless Las Vegas casino filled with silent gamblers and noisy slot machines, [Leo] staked me to a fifty-dollar bucket of coins," Steinem wrote. "After a couple of hours of twirling fruits and no idea what I was doing, I'd multiplied our money by five. Only then did he confess this had been his last fifty dollars." Steinem was lucky after all.

On the road home, father and daughter practiced their well-rehearsed childhood routines, buying and selling antique jewelry. Steinem put on jewelry that her father was trying to sell, and Leo acted as if the customers were getting real bargains because they were buying family heirlooms. "It was the same technique he had used on condescending antique[s] dealers in my childhood," Steinem said.

Eventually, the pair made it to New York City.

When they arrived, Steinem no longer felt the lure of Blair Chotzinoff. At that point she still assumed that she would someday settle down and have a family, but not yet. She wanted to work and support herself and live independently. She was ready to launch her career in journalism.

A drawing of a pin celebrating the 1959
World Youth Festival in Vienna
[Jess Magoo]

CHAPTER 8

THE CIA
CONNECTION

I was mostly trying to earn a living.

— GLORIA STEINEM

W hen Gloria Steinem returned to the United States in 1958, she was eager to talk about what she had seen and learned in India, but most people didn't have much interest in hearing about her experiences. "If I brought up India, an island of polite silence would appear in the conversation—and then the talk would flow right on around it," she said. While her heart remained in India, she realized that she lived in New York City now, so she stopped bringing up the topic and focused on finding work.

Steinem spent her days looking for assignments as a freelance writer, and she spent her nights sleeping on the living room floor in the apartment of a college friend. She answered dozens of newspaper ads for editorial positions, but she received one rejection after another. She needed a job. Any job. "I'm afraid the idealism with which I came back from India had been kind of squashed out of me," Steinem said. "I think I was mostly trying to earn a living."

While in Delhi, Steinem had met Clive Gray, who said he was in India working on his dissertation. Gray didn't mention that he was also working with the Central Intelligence Agency (CIA). His mission was to identify and develop relationships with up-and-coming foreign student leaders. Gray recognized something special in Steinem; he found her to be perceptive, intelligent, and hardworking. Unbeknownst to Steinem, he offered her name to the CIA as someone who might be considered for a job organizing American involvement in an upcoming international youth festival in Vienna, Austria, in the summer of 1959.

Gray followed up with Gloria when she returned to the United States. He offered her a job doing public relations work for a group known as the Independent Research Service. The group planned to send American students to an international communist youth festival, not to act as spies but to promote democratic ideals as an alternative to Communism.

Student political gatherings were nothing new. Since the end of World War II, students had been participating in international political meetings, including those involving Communism. In 1946, the International Union of Students held its first World Student Congress in Prague, Czechoslovakia, and twenty-five American students paid their own way to attend the meeting. The Americans found it appalling that the Soviet Union controlled the rhetoric in support of a pro-Communist agenda.

In response, in 1947 they formed their own group, the National Student Association, to promote democratic ideals. The National Student Association represented students from almost three hundred colleges and universities; it took positions on national issues of interest to young people, such as lowering the voting age to eighteen and supporting desegregation in American schools. In addition, the group had a travel bureau and sent students overseas to represent the United States at international conferences and festivals, as well as United Nations events. Many people believed that the best way to combat the spread of Communism was to show democracy in action, as represented by educated young Americans who were free to speak their minds.

They weren't the only anti-Communist voices: Students in other countries also formed anti-Communist organizations, and in 1950 these groups combined forces to form the International Student Conference, a coalition of international student groups that opposed Communism.

Why did this matter? These two groups — the pro-Communist International Union of Students and the anti-Communist International Student Conference — were both trying to win the allegiance of young people in developing countries who were just emerging from colonialism. The United States feared the spread of Communism. Many leaders believed that convincing the student leaders in these developing countries that democracy offered the promise of freedom and prosperity could go a long way toward building a democratic future for the world.

Even those who supported democracy had to admit that the Soviets and pro-Communists had some strong talking points. First, the Soviet group argued that they opposed colonialism, while the Western democracies who were now talking about freedom had until recently been their oppressors. They could also speak in lofty and idealistic terms about Marxism, and contrast that with the selfishness and greed of the capitalist system. In addition, the pro-Communist group was well organized and well financed because it had the backing of the Soviet state.

Rather than allow the Communists to control the message, the CIA decided to get involved to push a pro-democracy agenda. Behind the scenes, in 1951 the agency began providing funding and support to the National Student Association's international activities. The money was provided indirectly through a New York–based group called the Foundation for Youth and Student Affairs. The CIA didn't control the student group, but it did underwrite the budget so that students from democratic countries could be represented at the international gatherings. The goal was to counter Soviet propaganda with American propaganda and to spread the message of the virtues of freedom and democracy in the United States. Steinem later came to recognize the problems associated with patriarchy and capitalism, but she always favored freedom and democracy.

Very few students knew about the ties between the National

Student Association and the CIA. Only the president and the international vice president of the organization were let in on the secret; when they were told about the CIA connection, they were then given the opportunity to resign without getting involved. None of the student leaders objected to having CIA support because at the time the organization had a positive reputation with the public.

Once informed about the support of the CIA, these top student leaders were given a one-day class in how to avoid Soviet spies. They learned how to check light bulbs for wiretaps and how to completely destroy documents by burning them in an ashtray, stirring the ashes, and flushing them down the toilet. Most bugging equipment was very primitive, so they were told to go into the bathroom and run water in the background if they were having an important conversation because the equipment used to eavesdrop on conversations didn't work well with running water as background noise.

· · · · · · · ·

STEINEM DIDN'T KNOW anything about the connection between the CIA and the student groups. She was never trained in novice spy craft. When Clive Gray contacted Steinem, he told her that some former National Student Association people were establishing a new organization to send young people to international festivals to represent the face of democracy. Through their various social connections, he knew Steinem was looking for work, and he offered to introduce her to other officers in the organization.

Even though she had never attended any of the political festivals, Steinem was aware of them. She had considered attending the

1957 event in Moscow, but she decided not to go when the group of Indian friends she was traveling with were unable to make it. She was intrigued by Gray's offer because she was interested in attending the 1959 festival in Vienna, Austria.

After several interviews, Gray offered Steinem a job as director of the Independent Research Service/co–executive director of the Independent Service for Information on the Vienna Youth Festival. Her job would be public relations, including generating press coverage for the event and writing publications both before and after the festival. She would also recruit students to attend.

At first, Steinem had reservations about the job. The country was still recovering from the McCarthy-era, anti-Communist frenzy, and she worried that students attending the conference could experience backlash and accusations of being pro-Communist. She had concerns that the students who attended might be blocked from future government employment or that the Federal Bureau of Investigations (FBI) would open files on them. Still, she supported the idea of promoting democracy abroad and thought the work was important—she also didn't have any other job offers as a writer—so she accepted the position.

When she took the job, Steinem didn't know—and hadn't been told—anything about the Independent Research Service receiving financial support from the CIA. She may not have objected to CIA backing, even if she had been aware of it. At the time, she "remembers feeling relief that someone understood the importance of the non-Communist left in general, and students in particular." Widespread distrust of the CIA did not come until years later, when the public learned about clandestine operations to overthrow governments and topple individual leaders.

Steinem moved to Cambridge, Massachusetts, where the Independent Research Service was located. She lived in a basement apartment that reminded her of one of the rooms she shared with her mother in Toledo. She felt lonely and unwelcomed by the Harvard community that dominated Cambridge. Instead of participating in the social scene, she focused on her work promoting and publicizing the Austria event, letting students know that the festival was open to people with a range of political beliefs.

In July 1959, Steinem attended the ten-day festival, which included political discussions and workshops, as well as cultural events, such as ballet, opera, parades, and fireworks displays. Steinem ran the press bureau, writing press releases and lining up delegates for reporters to interview. Her goal was to support a free and open press corps.

During the festival, the Communists tried to isolate some of their representatives and performers so that they would not be exposed to the free expression of ideas demonstrated by the Americans and other Westerners. For example, members of a Leningrad ballet company were guarded at all times to prevent them from being influenced by dangerous outside ideas; even the windows on their buses were blocked so that they could not see out. Similarly, the Chinese delegates were kept away from Westerners; they could not even speak to the waiters who served at the restaurants where they ate their meals.

In fact, some of the delegates were trying to influence the pro-Communist delegates and performers. For example, some pro-Communist delegates were taken by bus to the Hungarian border with Austria to see the watchtowers and barbed-wire fences that were used to keep the Hungarians from escaping. Why would these extreme measures be necessary if the Hungarian people were satisfied with Communism?

In the months after the festival, Steinem compiled a final report about the event. This officially completed her assignment with the Independent Research Service. After submitting the final paper, she returned to New York City to look for work as a writer. This time her luck would be different.

LEO STEINEM

A portrait of Leo Steinem
[Jess Magoo]

CHAPTER 9

LEO'S DEATH

The cars are coming too fast to stop.

—Leo Steinem

When she was growing up, Gloria Steinem's father often warned her: "If we're ever in an accident on a freeway, get out and run—the cars are coming too fast to stop." Leo spent much of his life on the road—after his divorce, he essentially lived in his car—and he had a real appreciation of the damage that could be done in a traffic accident.

In April 1961, his words took on new meaning.

No one knows exactly what happened: Leo may have fallen asleep at the wheel, or another car may have drifted into his lane. What is known is that on a freeway in Orange County, California, Leo's car was sideswiped with such force that it spun in circles, directly into the path of oncoming traffic. Due to his size, he was pinned under the steering wheel and could not escape. A moment later, he was hit again from the opposite direction, compounding his injuries.

Leo was taken to an Orange County hospital. He was banged up but conscious. When the staff asked him for a phone number so that they could contact his family, Leo gave them Gloria's number, because Susanne had young children at home and Ruth wasn't capable of traveling to see him. Unfortunately, Gloria was out of the country and would not return for several days.

In the meantime, the hospital had followed up with Susanne, who called her sister at the hotel in the Caribbean where she was vacationing. Together, the family—Gloria, Susanne, and Ruth—decided that it would be best for Gloria to go to California in about a week, when Leo was expected to be transferred from the hospital to a long-term-care center. Susanne had four young children at the time and could not travel.

"I think I sensed that I should go right away, yet somehow the accident seemed like a normal part of my father's life on the road, nothing to be too alarmed about," Gloria wrote. She tried to downplay her anxiety, but Gloria had another worry: She feared that if she went to California, she would be forced to become her father's caretaker—just as she had taken care of her mother—and she would never get to return to her own life.

A few days later, the doctor called to report that Leo was in serious condition due to unexpected internal bleeding. Gloria immediately flew to Los Angeles, but when she reached Chicago to change planes, she heard her name announced over the loudspeaker. She called her sister, who said that Leo had experienced a massive hemorrhage and died. It was four days before his sixty-fourth birthday.

Gloria went on to the hospital to settle her father's affairs. "When I arrived at the hospital, I found only a manila envelope with my father's few belongings and a doctor who seemed barely able to control his anger that no family member had been present," Gloria wrote. The doctor told her that her father had died from bleeding ulcers, which proved more lethal than his crash wounds. "I don't know whether I was listening with a daughter's ears or hearing a fact, but I thought he was saying that this fatal bleeding had been caused not by the crash itself, but by trauma, stress, despair," Gloria wrote. She felt guilty that she hadn't made it to her father's bedside before he died.

Leo's body was cremated, and his ashes were sent back to Washington, DC, where the family held a memorial service. "I will never stop wishing I had been with him," said Gloria, who was twenty-seven years old when her father died.

In the years before the accident, Gloria had visited with her father less frequently. She took for granted that they would have more time, and so she let too many things go unsaid. She never told him how thankful she was that her father had stopped at horse farms and taken her on pony rides when she was a horse-crazy young girl. She never told him how much she appreciated his optimistic outlook: As her father always said, "If I don't know what will happen tomorrow, it could be wonderful!" She never told him how grateful she was that he respected her ability to think for herself. Gloria recalled a time she saw her best friend's father demand that her friend eat every bite on her plate before getting dessert. When she got home, Gloria decided to test her father by asking for dessert, pointing out that she hadn't finished her meal. "'That's okay,' he said. 'Sometimes you're hungry for one thing and not another.' I loved him so much at that moment," she said.

Years later, Gloria recognized that having a loving and supportive father actually changed the nature of her future relationships with men. "Only after I saw women who were attracted to distant, condescending, even violent men did I begin to understand that having a distant, condescending, even violent father could make those qualities seem inevitable, even feel like home," she said. "Because of my father, only kindness felt like home." Her father taught her through his example that she deserved to be in a relationship with a kind and loving man.

• • • • • • • •

DECADES AFTER HER father died, Gloria received unsolicited letters from two men who had known her father. The first letter came from a retired doctor who had spent a summer as a trombone player with the house band at Ocean Beach Pier. One night the bandleader stole all their money and left, leaving the young man and his friend penniless and stranded. "Your father saved the summer for us by offering us a place to stay and enough cash to help us get food," he wrote. Leo housed the boys and he arranged for them to have day jobs at a cement-block manufacturing plant nearby. This letter was a witness to her father's kindness. "My father knew a good heart when he saw one," Gloria said.

The second letter came from another retired physician, one who was the son of a man who considered Leo his best friend. "I never saw my dad happier than when he was around Leo," the man wrote. "Being a pal of Leo's was the best. He treated everyone equally, he was not pretentious nor condescending. He was kind. And best of all, he was fun. He had lots of stories."

In his letter, the doctor said that he and his father had learned that Leo had been in a serious car accident. He wanted her to know that he and his father drove down to visit Leo in the intensive care unit of the hospital before he died. He was breathing through an oxygen mask and his body was bruised. "I wish I could remember all that was said," the doctor wrote. "But I guess it doesn't matter. The main thing was he knew he wasn't alone."

Gloria found great relief in those words. She had not been able to be with Leo when he died, but her father had not been alone.

Gloria Steinem in New York City
{Bettmann/Getty Images}

CHAPTER 10

FREELANCE
WRITER

For me, writing is the only thing that passes the three tests of métier:
(1) when I'm doing it, I don't feel that I should be doing something else
instead; (2) it produces a sense of accomplishment and, once in a while,
pride; and (3) it's frightening.

— GLORIA STEINEM

lthough she was devastated by her father's death, Gloria
Steinem returned to New York City to continue with her
freelance writing career. She had rented an apartment
across from the Museum of Natural History on West Eighty-First
Street and continued looking for work. She got her first break
when she was introduced to Harvey Kurtzman—the friend of a

friend—who had created *Mad* magazine nine years earlier. He had just launched a new satirical magazine called *Help! For Tired Minds*, and he needed someone to write funny captions, coordinate photo shoots, and reach out to famous people and ask them to appear on the cover and in photos in the comic strips. Kurtzman liked Steinem, so he hired her part-time, two days a week.

Steinem began dating Robert Benton, the assistant art director at *Esquire* magazine, and she spent a lot of time at his office when she wasn't working. *Esquire* published a new style of writing—what would later be called New Journalism—a style of nonfiction that used narrative, scenes, and dialogue to create lively prose. She volunteered to help out at the magazine when needed, and she earned her first bylined piece in the July 1961 issue.

In late 1961, Clive Gray called Steinem and asked if she might be interested in working at the Ninth Youth Festival in Helsinki, Finland, in 1962. Steinem didn't want to give up her freelance career, so she agreed to work part-time. The main office of the Independent Research Service had moved to New York, so Steinem could stay in the city and continue with her writing. During the festival, Steinem spent a lot of time working on a daily pro-democracy newspaper published by Finnish student groups to counter the official newspaper of the festival, which had a pro-Communist slant. When she returned to the United States, Steinem wrote a short piece about the festival for the October 1962 issue of *Show* magazine.

Steinem spent so much time at the *Esquire* office that she got to know the staff, including features editor Clay Felker, who became a very important person in her career. Felker suggested that Steinem write an article about how the birth control pill was changing sexual behavior on college campuses. This would be her first major assignment, and she meticulously researched the topic. The article she wrote included lots of statistics and details, but not a lot of passion or spirit. When she submitted the work, Felker told her, "Congratulations. You've managed to make sex dull."

Steinem didn't lose heart. She tirelessly rewrote the article until it was published as "The Moral Disarmament of Betty Coed" in the September 1962 issue of *Esquire*.

With that article to her credit, Steinem began to get assignments at other magazines. Like other women writers, most of the articles assigned to her were about food, fashion, or family—the topics considered appropriate for female journalists. It was assumed that women were experts on themselves—and almost nothing else. All other topics belonged to men. Steinem asked people to imagine if the situation were reversed and men could write about hunting, shaving, and paternity—and nothing else.

Steinem wanted to write serious articles about political topics and social justice, but these assignments went to her male colleagues, even if she had more impressive credentials than they did. At that point, the editors at *Esquire* and *Show* knew that they could count on Steinem, and they began to assign her celebrity profiles—not just fluff pieces, but more complex and thoughtful portraits of well-known figures. She earned a reputation for turning in good work, on time, and at the assigned word count. Before long she got assignments from the *New York Times* and magazines such as *Glamour, Ladies' Home Journal,* and *Harper's*. She profiled well-known writers, such as Dorothy Parker and Truman Capote, as well as entertainers, such as Paul Newman and Barbra Streisand.

Steinem loved the life of a freelance writer. Her father had equipped her well with the confidence to live with the unpredictability of erratic work. And she found the writer's life rewarding, if difficult. "For me," she wrote, "writing is the only thing that passes the three tests of métier: (1) when I'm doing it, I don't feel that I should be doing something else instead; (2) it produces a sense of accomplishment and, once in a while, pride; and (3) it's frightening."

• • • • • • • •

AS THE MONTHS PASSED, the relationship between Steinem and Benton became serious. Although she had been engaged to marry Blair Chotzinoff seven years earlier, in hindsight Steinem said that she considered her affair with Benton to be the first time she had really fallen in love because it was the first time she was with a man who shared her interests. "Blair was a kind, sexual, sensual, funny person, but we didn't share interests, so there was an awful lot of both of us that was left out of the picture," Steinem said. "But with Benton, we were totally in this relationship."

Benton encouraged Steinem to feel confident in who she was, telling her she didn't need to reinvent herself to fit into every social situation. In turn, Steinem encouraged Benton to develop his writing, which he did. Benton became a well-known writer and movie director, creating the films *Bonnie and Clyde*, *Kramer vs. Kramer*, and *Places in the Heart*; he won three Academy Awards, for Best Director, Best Original Screenplay, and Best Adapted Screenplay. They trusted each other and shared the truth about their childhood vulnerabilities. With Benton, Steinem felt free to be her uncensored self.

They had a playful side, too. Steinem enjoyed partying with Benton's friends from Texas, including writers Liz Smith and

Harvey Schmidt, and singer Tom Jones. The group sometimes stayed out all night or woke up early and played croquet in Central Park and then went to lunch at the Plaza Hotel.

After dating for a year and a half, Steinem and Benton talked about getting married. Once again, she had reservations about losing herself inside a marriage. She said she didn't mind compromising, but she didn't want to give up her professional life, her name, and her identity. "It wasn't just compromise," she said. "It was surrender."

Because Steinem was wary of commitment, they moved their plans forward one step at a time. "The first was to do the blood tests and get the license," she said. "We did." Next, Benton bought a new suit. The third step was for Steinem to buy a wedding dress. "I never got to the dress," she said. "I just couldn't do it, and the marriage license expired."

Steinem didn't want to give up the relationship, but she didn't want to move it forward, either. She wanted to hold on to the status quo, to leave things the way they were for a while. They stayed together for a while, as Steinem focused on her career. She was beginning to get more lucrative and prestigious writing assignments, but she had no idea she was about to write an article that would make her a household name.

Gloria Steinem in her Playboy Bunny costume. August 1960
[Bettman/Getty Images]

CHAPTER 11

BUNNY

All women are Bunnies.

—GLORIA STEINEM

The ad asked a simple question: "Do Playboy Club Bunnies Really Have Glamorous Jobs, Meet Celebrities, and Make Top Money?" Before readers had a chance to ponder the issue, the too-good-to-be-true solicitation offered an answer: "Yes, it's true!" The ad promised that attractive young girls could earn $200 to $300 a week working at the New York Playboy Club.

In addition to enjoying "the glamorous and exciting aura of show business," the women would have the opportunity to travel to other Playboy Clubs throughout the world.

Not just any girl would do: The ad specified that prospective applicants needed to be attractive and twenty-one to twenty-four years old. They were told to bring a swimsuit or leotard with them for an in-person interview.

Hugh Hefner, the publisher of *Playboy* magazine, was about to open a Playboy Club in New York City. His magazine featured photographs of naked and almost-naked women, and the clubs were an attempt to give readers a chance to live out some of their fantasies by attending a club where the waitresses dressed in skimpy costumes as Playboy Bunnies.

The editors at *Show* had seen the ads and wanted to find a creative way to cover the story. At an editorial meeting to discuss story ideas for the upcoming issue, Steinem jokingly suggested that they hire a reporter to do an investigative piece by going undercover as a Playboy Bunny.

Instead of laughing her off, the editors looked at one another and then at Steinem. They liked the idea, and they wanted Steinem to be the one to go undercover. She was young, attractive, and eager to get a major assignment.

With more than a few reservations, Steinem agreed. She didn't think the assignment would go too far, since she was four years over the age limit of twenty-four, and she knew she'd have to show identification, since New York State required proof of age for anyone who served liquor. As she thought through the logistics of how to go undercover, she remembered that she had saved her grandmother's Social Security card when she died, so she figured she would apply for the job using the name of her maternal grandmother, Marie Catherine Ochs. "It sounds much too square to be phony," Steinem said.

She didn't think she'd get the job. She assumed she would go in for an audition and that would become the heart of the story. "I went, and the thing took on a life of its own," she said.

Steinem worked out her backstory and went to apply for the job. No one asked about the details of her life: All she had to share was her address, phone number, measurements, age, and last three employers.

More important than her work experience was how she looked in a Bunny suit. The "wardrobe mistress" handed Steinem a bright blue satin costume and told her to put it on. "It was so tight that the zipper caught my skin as she fastened the back," Steinem wrote in the article she first published in *Show* magazine. "She told me to inhale as she zipped again." The wardrobe attendant looked her over. The leg openings were cut up so high in the front that Steinem's hip bones were exposed, and in the back the costume revealed "a good five inches of untanned derrière." The woman stuffed an entire plastic dry-cleaning bag into the top of Steinem's costume to make her breasts appear larger. "The whole costume was darted and seamed until it was two inches smaller than any of my measurements everywhere except the bust," Steinem wrote.

"The costume was so tight, it would have given a man cleavage," she said.

Steinem was issued two costumes, blue and orange. She was told to buy two pairs of three-inch satin heels and dye them to match.

Before starting work, she was told to come back for a makeup lesson (including the use of false eyelashes), to study her copy of the Playboy Club Bunny bible, and to go to an appointment to see the doctor for a physical exam. The following Monday, the Playboy doctor gave Steinem a blood test for venereal disease and an internal vaginal exam. "Is that required of waitresses in New York State?" Steinem asked the doctor.

"What do you care?" he said. "It's free, and it's for everybody's good."

"How?" she asked.

"Look," he said. "We usually find that girls who object to it strenuously have some reason . . ." Steinem knew she could not object too strongly or she would lose the job—and possibly the story. She allowed the doctor to complete the exam.

Steinem called the Board of Health after leaving the doctor's office. She asked what medical exams were required to work as a waitress.

The answer: None at all.

• • • • • • • •

ON HER FIRST night on the job as a Bunny, Steinem started in the hat-check room, working from 7:30 p.m. to 4:00 a.m. By the end of her shift, her feet were throbbing.

"I went back to the Bunny room, turned in my costume, and sat motionless, too tired to move," Steinem wrote. The costume had made red marks around her rib cage, and the zipper had left an impression over her spine. She complained about the costume's tightness to the Bunny who was sitting next to her. "Yeah," the exhausted Bunny said. "A lot of girls say their legs get numb from the knee up. I think it presses on a nerve or something."

The dehumanization was taken for granted. The women— "girls"—were there to fulfill the fantasies of men they did not know; they were objects—sexualized "Bunnies"—not human beings worthy of respect. Most of the women were white, but they had some minorities. "The men call colored girls Chocolate Bunnies," Steinem said.

Steinem returned to the club the following afternoon and began a shift as a waitress. A week of unpaid training, followed by a week as a regular Bunny, was all that Steinem could take. The experience of wearing high heels for long hours while carrying heavy trays left her feet a half size larger than before she took the job. She had also lost ten pounds.

"Somehow, the usual tail-pullings and propositions and pinching and ogling seemed all the more depressing when, outside this windowless room of perpetual night, the sun was shining," Steinem wrote on her last day on the job. As soon as she thought she had enough information for her story, she told her supervisor that her mother was ill and she had to go home for a while. She collected a paycheck: $35.90 for two exhausting nights of work. When she asked about the night she worked hat-check, she was told that she wouldn't be paid because that was considered training.

Show magazine published the two-part article, "A Bunny's Tale: *Show*'s First Exposé for Intelligent People," in the May and June issues of 1963. Steinem thought the articles would discourage women from wanting to be Bunnies, but some readers wrote to her trying to get more information about how to become Bunnies.

One woman wrote: "Dear Miss Steinem: I happen to be a great admirer of yours, and although this request is probably unusual, I do hope you will answer my questions. At some time in the past, I read that you had been a 'Playboy Bunny.' I am interested in becoming one but I don't know how to go about it."

Steinem wrote back: "I'm afraid I can't honestly encourage your interest in becoming a Playboy Bunny . . . At best, you are a glorified waitress, and at worst a sort of Pop geisha who is encouraged to go out with anybody who could do the club any good . . . it was still one of the two or three most depressing experiences of my life."

· · · · · · · ·

HUGH HEFNER FILED a one-million-dollar libel lawsuit against Steinem and a small New York newspaper that quoted her article and alleged that the club had connections to organized crime. (Steinem did not mention organized crime in her article.) Hefner lost the lawsuit, but Steinem had to pay the cost of defending herself in court. She countersued and won back her court costs and expenses. Still, Hefner got what he wanted: The fear of lawsuits stopped many publications from writing unfavorable articles about the Playboy Clubs. There was one positive change: In response to the unwelcome attention, Hefner did stop conducting the physical exams for Bunny applicants.

After the Bunny article appeared, Steinem found that she stopped getting serious journalistic assignments. Although she saw the story as a meaningful look at the systematic exploitation of women, editors acted as if the story undermined her legitimacy as a writer. Editors asked her to do articles about going undercover as a call girl or prostitute; she turned them down in disgust.

For many years, Steinem considered writing the article a mistake. When a reporter challenged her, arguing, "That piece put you on the map," without hesitation, Steinem said, "Well, it was the wrong map."

In time, Steinem changed her mind about the story. "After feminism arrived in my life, I stopped regretting that I had written this article," she wrote. When she saw the article in a feminist context, she had a deeper appreciation for what she had achieved. Twenty years after it first appeared, Steinem reprinted the article in her first book, *Outrageous Acts and Everyday Rebellions*. By that point, she saw it differently. Upon further reflection, she realized that "all women are Bunnies." She saw the piece as a story about working conditions and a community of women supporting one another as they tried to get through the challenges of life on the job.

Steinem didn't back down. She continued to pitch serious story ideas and write about topics that interested her. She ignored her critics and kept working. She wasn't going anywhere.

Gloria Steinem, photographed in July 1965
[Yale Joel/The LIFE Picture Collection via Getty Images]

CHAPTER 12

OUTSIDER

I'll definitely get married, *I kept thinking,* but not right now. There's this one thing I want to do first . . .

— GLORIA STEINEM

Gloria Steinem wasn't just a writer. After the Playboy Bunny article, she became something of a celebrity herself. In the mid-1960s, Steinem appeared frequently in the press—not with a byline but as the subject of a number of newspaper and magazine articles.

Writer Nora Ephron interviewed Steinem for a January 1964

article in the *New York Post* about posing as a Playboy Bunny. At that point, Steinem had been receiving a lot of attention about the article, but she wanted to be recognized for more than one story. "There are people who know me only for having done the Bunny piece," she said. "I am constantly being referred to as an ex-Bunny, and that's a high price to pay." Ephron presented Steinem in a more complex and multidimensional way.

Steinem proved to be an interesting subject, one who defied easy categorization. She was a Phi Beta Kappa, a magna cum laude Smith graduate who was known for her miniskirts, boyfriends, and her presence on the New York City social scene. She had proven herself as a dedicated and competent writer with a respectable résumé, but many editors still dismissed her as a lightweight, less-than-serious writer. She embodied what had been considered mutually exclusive ideas of femaleness—beauty and brains, sexuality and smarts, ambition and tradition—challenging conventional expectations of what it meant to be female.

The press loved her, at least in the beginning. Articles in *Glamour*, *Vogue*, *Harper's Bazaar*, *Women's Wear Daily*, *Newsweek*, *Ladies' Home Journal*, and *Newsday* followed Ephron's *New York Post* story, typically discussing Steinem's personal style and clothes. By May 1965, however, the press coverage developed a sharper edge. That month *Newsweek* published a short piece about Steinem titled "News Girl," which read: "Usually the journalist remembers his place—on the edge of the action recording the news made by others. But Gloria Steinem, a striking brunette of thirty, is as much a celebrity as a reporter and often generates news in her own right." A photograph accompanying the text showed Steinem posed in a chair, holding a cigarette in the air, with her short skirt riding up her thighs. The caption read: "Steinem: Easier than you think." The "easy" comment was supposed to refer to a remark she made about freelance writing, but the innuendo was obvious. Steinem was embarrassed and hurt by the article. She complained to the writer who had interviewed her, and he apologized and explained that he had been on vacation and someone else wrote the caption.

Steinem not only wrote about famous subjects, she also befriended them. Steinem attended Truman Capote's November 1966 infamous masquerade party at the Plaza Hotel known as the Black and White Ball. The *Washington Post* called the guest list a "Who's Who of the World," including movie stars, politicians, artists, socialites, and other people Capote liked or considered important. Steinem made the list.

It was not long before Steinem was considered not only beautiful but also one of "the Beautiful People." Former *New York Times* reporter Marylin Bender included Steinem in her book, *The Beautiful People*, writing: "Miss Steinem swings with the new society despite the fact that she is what used to be called whistle-bait. . . . She also earns her own living, has a Phi Beta Kappa key and has evidenced more than casual interest in politics and civil rights."

Despite this clear sign of social acceptance, Steinem didn't feel she fit in. To the rest of the world, she may have looked like an insider—witty and charming, often invited to the fun and fashionable parties of the day—but she felt like an outsider. She later admitted that during this time in her life she felt like a pretender, a poseur, especially at large gatherings.

She remained adept at reading social cues and adapting to new situations, a skill she had cultivated in her childhood. She watched what other people did and followed with an air of confidence, just as she had been doing since her time in Toledo. She learned which fork to use at a gala dinner and how to make small talk at elegant parties. "It's amazing how fast you can learn because you're scared—so you absorb this knowledge very quickly," she said.

Steinem may have socialized with the wealthy, but she remained a freelance writer who often struggled to make ends meet. She attended fancy dinners and society parties, but like Cinderella after the ball, when the party was over she returned to a rent-controlled, $125-a-month, twenty-by-twenty-five-foot studio apartment she shared with artist Barbara Nessim. The space was so small that she never fully unpacked her boxes. The cramped quarters didn't really bother Steinem, who had become comfortable in crowded conditions when she lived with her mother in Toledo.

Nessim and Steinem got along well as roommates, moving to an apartment on West Fifty-Sixth Street and then to a brownstone on East Seventy-Third. In 1968 Nessim moved out and got a place of her own, but she and Steinem remained friends.

· · · · · · · ·

AT THIS TIME in her life, Steinem still expected to live a traditional life and have a conventional marriage. Each time she started a new relationship, she wondered if it would be the one to make her want to settle down for good. Later Steinem remembered "trying on the name and life of each man I thought I might marry."

Like most women of her generation, she wasn't sure what her life would look like if she didn't marry and have children. "[I] thought I would *have* to marry eventually if I was to be a whole person," she said. *"I'll definitely get married,* I kept thinking, *but not right now. There's this one thing I want to do first . . ."*

For the most part, Steinem dated one man at a time. After she ended her relationship with Robert Benton, she began seeing Tom Guinzburg, the publisher at Viking Press. (Guinzburg published her first book, *The Beach Book,* a playful collection of lighthearted pieces related to the beach.) Guinzburg helped Steinem break into the social circuit by introducing her to New York's intellectuals and show-business elite.

Next, she went out with film and theater director and producer Mike Nichols, who had just won a Tony Award for the Broadway play *Barefoot in the Park.* A number of friends tried to talk her into marrying Nichols, and for a time she tried to talk herself into it as well. She was thirty years old, and she still assumed that she would marry and start a family.

But marriage still didn't feel right for Steinem. When she and Nichols went to dinner parties together, Steinem didn't feel that she was recognized as her own person. At these events, she was not Gloria Steinem, she was Mike Nichols's girlfriend. While she respected and admired his work, she didn't want to exist in his shadow; she had ambitions of her own, and she didn't want to be defined by someone else, anyone else. If they married—if she became Mrs. Mike Nichols—she wasn't sure she would ever get the chance to feel whole and independent again.

Ultimately, this relationship ended, too. She then dated writer Herb Sargent, who had hired her to write for his live television program *That Was the Week That Was,* which featured short, satirical skits, not unlike *Saturday Night Live.* As a couple, Steinem and

Sargent spent a lot of time at Elaine's, a restaurant on the Upper East Side that was famous at the time for attracting celebrities.

For the most part, she found these relationships, which she called "little marriages," satisfying and meaningful. She always kept her own apartment, but she often spent weekends and vacations with her partners. She learned that she didn't need to marry to have a man in her life, and when the relationships ended, most evolved into lifelong friendships. It was not until the late 1970s that Steinem let go of the idea that she would marry.

Some people accused Steinem of choosing and using lovers who would further her ambitions. "I used to seek out rich and famous men," Steinem said. "Not to the extent of going out with somebody I didn't like, but it used to matter to me." While many of the men she dated did help her career, she insisted she only dated men she cared about.

While Steinem continued to search for emotional fulfillment in her private life, her life wasn't all glitz and love affairs. During the 1960s she became increasingly involved in social movements, protesting against the war in Vietnam and in favor of civil rights and improved working conditions for migrant farmworkers. She organized fund-raisers and attended rallies and protest marches.

Steinem wasn't shy about using her social status to promote the causes she considered worthy. She asked her wealthy friends for money and spoke out about the issues of the day—such as the war in Vietnam—becoming the voice and the conscience of the liberal "in" group in New York City. Steinem's world was opening up, but what she really wanted was the chance to write about the issues she cared about.

Diane Von Furstenberg, Gloria Steinem,
Bella Abzug, and Barbra Streisand
[Globe Photos/MediaPunch/Alamy]

CHAPTER 13

COLUMNIST

For the first time, I wasn't writing about one thing while caring about something else.

—GLORIA STEINEM

G loria Steinem wanted respect as a serious writer. While she occasionally had the chance to cover political topics, too often she felt marginalized and dismissed as either irrelevant or incompetent. Her feelings were based on experience, not insecurity. Consider one example: When she was covering Robert Kennedy's run for the United States Senate in New York, she shared a taxi with two well-known writers—Gay Talese and Saul Bellow—who had attended the same political event. While squeezed into the back seat of the taxi, sandwiched between two men whose work she admired, Talese acted as if Steinem weren't in the car, leaned over, and said to Bellow, "You know how every year there's a pretty girl who comes to New York and pretends to be a writer? Well, Gloria is this year's pretty girl."

Steinem felt humiliated and angry. She didn't know how to respond; she felt invisible, so she acted invisible and said nothing, allowing them a laugh at her expense. Afterward, Steinem had time to think about her feelings. She vowed to use her anger to prove them wrong. The snide remark motivated her to redouble her efforts to excel as a journalist and activist.

She did not forget the remark or the way it made her feel. Steinem continued writing, and as her awareness of political issues grew, she began marching and protesting against the war in Vietnam and in favor of a nuclear-test-ban treaty. She joined the 1961 Women Strike for Peace protest, in which twenty-five hundred women stormed the Pentagon and demanded to see the generals who were making decisions about the war in Vietnam. The protesters carried signs reading CHILDREN ARE NOT FOR BURNING that featured gruesome photographs of napalmed Vietnamese children.

"We all demonstrated outside the Pentagon," Steinem said. In response to the protest, the women were ushered into an auditorium to meet with members of Congress. "Of course, the only members who would come were people who agreed with us already," she said.

It was at that protest that Steinem met Bella Abzug, one of the spokeswomen for the protest, who would later become a congresswoman from New York. "Bella was leading the presentation," Steinem said. "And she scared the shit out of me. She was just so aggressive—assertive doesn't do it." Abzug's forwardness offended New York senator Jacob Javits, but he still supported the protesters. "I will oppose the war *in spite* of you," Javits told Abzug.

Steinem also felt assaulted by Abzug's tone, at least at first. "I had never seen a woman being that out there," Steinem said. "I was very, very put off by it. It was not a good experience." A few weeks later, Steinem spent time with Abzug at another organizing meeting, and she began to appreciate Abzug's style and passion for justice. "Gradually I began to realize that my response to her was my problem, not hers. If I was afraid to see Bella being a whole person, anger and all, that was because I was still afraid to be a whole person myself."

· · · · · · · ·

IN 1968, Steinem finally got a forum to raise her voice and speak her mind. That year Clay Felker, who had been one of Steinem's editors at *Esquire* and had remained a close friend, started *New York*, a monthly magazine dedicated to reporting on issues of interest to people living in New York City. Steinem's work experience and social connections helped her career advancement. Felker offered Steinem a position as a contributing editor and political columnist.

In her column, the City Politic, Steinem wrote about the Vietnam War, civil rights, political campaigns, or anything else that inspired her. "For the first time, I wasn't writing about one thing while caring about something else," Steinem said. She wasn't just reporting what other people had to say about issues, she was part of the conversation.

There was plenty to write about in 1968. Just after the first issue of *New York* appeared on the newsstands, Rev. Martin Luther King Jr. was assassinated. Riots broke out in one hundred cities across the country. Steinem was in her apartment trying to make sense of the news when Felker called her.

"What are you doing in your apartment?" he asked. "You call yourself a reporter? Get up to Harlem and interview people and see what they're saying." Steinem spent the next few days shadowing New York mayor John Lindsay and talking with people in Black neighborhoods. She wrote a column arguing that New York City may have avoided the riots that shook other cities because the mayor went into the African American community and met with the leaders there during the crisis.

The pace of political upheaval did not let up. The nation grieved again when Senator Robert Kennedy was assassinated in June. His death left the Democratic Party scrambling to shake out its presidential politics before the Democratic National Convention in Chicago two months later. Steinem had been covering the campaign of antiwar Democratic presidential candidate Minnesota senator Eugene McCarthy, but she wasn't enthusiastic in her support. She wanted to like him, but she found him condescending and dull.

She also had questions about the way McCarthy treated the women working in his campaign. "Like other women, I had either stayed at the edges doing menial jobs or been hidden away in some back room," Steinem said. She came to understand that this was done for one of two reasons: because the campaign didn't want to acknowledge that a woman was working on speeches and policy decisions, or because someone might assume she was having an affair with the candidate.

When Senator George McGovern joined the presidential race in August 1968, Steinem shifted her support to him. He opposed the war and also supported a more progressive agenda. She worked on his campaign, writing fund-raising letters and handling publicity. Steinem had a knack for coming up with sound bites. During an interview on a late-night radio talk show, Steinem said, "George McGovern is the real Eugene McCarthy." This became a popular campaign slogan.

The 1968 Democratic Convention proved to be famously contentious. Antiwar demonstrators protested outside the hall, and Chicago police used tear gas and physical force to control them. More than one hundred protesters were hospitalized with injuries. While most of the disruption occurred outside, some of the disorder did spill over into the convention itself. Steinem got caught up in some of the push and pull while she was passing out literature for the United Farm Workers union. "I was distributing literature on the floor when the [Chicago mayor Richard] Daley guards shoved me aside and broke my glasses," Steinem said.

Steinem's front-seat involvement in these efforts legitimized her status as a political writer. She offered a first-person view of what was happening inside politics. McGovern lost the 1968 Democratic nomination to Hubert Humphrey, but he had learned a lot about how to be a national political candidate. After he lost the nomination, McGovern began to strategize about another run in 1972. He approached Steinem and asked her to take part in a meeting about the long-term planning for his next run, but his campaign manager, former Connecticut governor Abraham Ribicoff, uninvited her.

"No broads," Ribicoff said.

McGovern sheepishly told Steinem that he had tried to advocate for her, but Ribicoff remained steadfast. Clearly McGovern didn't try very hard; he was the candidate, after all. Steinem lost some respect for McGovern, noting that he would never have gone along if Ribicoff had said "No Blacks" or "No Jews."

In addition to presidential politics, Steinem covered the rising death count in Vietnam. In 1967, she joined the Writers and Editors War Tax Protest, signing a public declaration that she and several hundred others would not pay a 10 percent surcharge to the income tax to pay for the expenses of the Vietnam War. At first, those who signed weren't sure if they would face legal consequences, which could have been as much as one year in jail and a $10,000 fine. In the end, the Internal Revenue Service simply removed the funds from their bank accounts instead of prosecuting them.

While the tax protest may have ended with a fizzle, Steinem remained an advocate for social justice, using both her words and actions. She continued to work on other issues, but in the late 1960s she became increasingly involved with Cesar Chavez, migrant farmers, and the campaigns of the United Farm Workers.

Marion Moses, a nurse for the United Farm Workers union
[Bob Fitch/Stanford University. Department of Special Collections and
University Archives]

CHAPTER 14

UNITED FARM WORKERS

There are few rewards greater than uncovering a secret that shouldn't be a secret.

— GLORIA STEINEM

In 1968, Gloria Steinem got a call from a former college roommate asking for a favor: The friend wanted to know if Steinem would allow Marion Moses, a nurse from the United Farm Workers union, to sleep on her couch. Steinem agreed and then offered Moses much more than a place to sleep.

Moses was in New York organizing a consumer boycott of

table grapes as part of a campaign to bring attention to the plight of migrant farmworkers. Migrant laborers worked ten to twelve hours a day, six or seven days a week, for extremely low wages. To make matters worse, they were also exposed to toxic pesticides and forced to work with little or no access to toilets or clean drinking water in the fields.

It was challenging to advocate for improved conditions because the laws protecting workers did not apply to farmers. The employees—many of whom were poor seasonal workers from Mexico—hesitated to complain because they knew they would be fired and replaced by others desperate enough to accept their jobs, even with lousy working conditions. The union wanted to draw attention to their cause by raising public consciousness about the farmworkers' harsh conditions. Union leader Cesar Chavez had studied the writings of Mahatma Gandhi, and he used nonviolent means to convince growers to recognize the farmworkers' union. He chose to focus on a boycott of table grapes because the delicate fruit had to be picked by hand; he did not target wine grapes because the wine grape growers used unionized pickers.

Moses had been working on the boycott campaign for several weeks, but she wasn't getting anywhere. She heard lots of words of sympathy and concern, but she didn't get much tangible support for her cause—until she connected with Steinem.

The two women met for lunch and hit it off. "Right away Marion's sense of urgency was contagious," Steinem wrote. Moses told Steinem what she needed, and they got to work.

In their meeting, Moses explained that the situation had become dangerous for migrant workers. "Two farmworkers with the union had been 'accidentally' run over in the fields, she explained, and two local California sheriffs had refused to investigate," Steinem later wrote. Acting as a reporter, Steinem called the sheriff's office asking if they had started an investigation, but the sheriff—who sided with the farm owners—ignored her and took no action.

Steinem wanted to do all she could to help. She invited Moses to stay at her home and provided connections to her friends in the media, as well as those who could help with fund-raising. They lined up interviews for articles in *Time*, *Life*, and *Look* magazines, as well as an appearance for union leader Cesar Chavez on the *Today* show.

Although she had reservations about participating, Steinem joined Moses on a picket line outside a New York City supermarket where grapes were sold. "I felt like an idiot," Steinem said. "I had to explain to skeptical New Yorkers that no, I wasn't a farmworker, I was a customer who didn't want to eat food that had been picked in poverty." Steinem and the other picketers passed out flyers explaining that the grape pickers received low wages for backbreaking work, and they were exposed to dangerous pesticides and unsanitary working conditions. When enough shoppers stopped by to listen to the protesters, the store owner allowed the bag boys to leave their posts and harass the picketers, yelling, "Honey, I'd like to press your grapes!"

As the boycott gained momentum, politicians got involved. Progressives supported the union, and conservatives backed the grape growers. President Richard Nixon said he planned to eat California grapes "whenever I can." To undermine the farmworkers and support the growers, Nixon also arranged for the military to buy grapes to send to the soldiers in Vietnam. California governor Ronald Reagan opposed the union organizers and called the farmworkers "barbarians."

· · · · · · · · ·

STEINEM MET CHAVEZ when he came to New York for a round of press interviews in May 1968. She was impressed with his commitment to *la causa*—the cause—and she soon agreed to work with Moses to organize a fund-raising benefit for the farmworkers at Carnegie Hall. The event raised $30,000, and it elevated the status of the movement.

The following year, Chavez asked Gloria for help again. This time the union needed assistance publicizing their next major event, a one-hundred-mile march from their headquarters in Delano, California, to Calexico, on the Mexican border, where they were to be met by farmworkers from Mexico. The goal was to promote international cooperation between the workers of Mexico and the United States. "Farmworkers from Mexico and California will meet in a massive rally at Calexico, a town whose very name is a blend of two countries, and declare that the poor of one country will no longer be used against the poor of another," Steinem wrote.

Steinem agreed to help, but it proved to be quite a challenge. Calexico was hours from the airport and the conditions were harsh: 110-degree days were not unusual. She worried that she would be unable to get reporters to put forth the effort required to make it to the site. "This historic event is like a tree falling in the forest with no one to hear," she wrote.

She knew she needed political or celebrity involvement to get press coverage. Senator Robert Kennedy had been assassinated in June 1968, and she didn't have another superstar politician to count on. After considerable effort, she lined up civil rights leader Rev. Ralph Abernathy and Senators Ted Kennedy, Walter Mondale, and John Tunney. Although it was difficult, the event generated the kind of buzz she had hoped it would. When she returned to New York, the taxi driver taking her home asked her where she had been and Steinem told him about the march. To her surprise, the driver said that he had heard about it. "I'm surprised by how much this means to me," she recalled. "There are few rewards greater than uncovering a secret that shouldn't be a secret."

• • • • • • • •

THE CALEXICO MARCH was Steinem's last major effort for the farmworkers' union. She respected Chavez and his nonviolent Gandhian approach to organizing, but she had concerns about the way he treated women. Chavez—a product of his time and his culture—did not see women as equals, and he did not respect women's rights to control their bodies.

In addition to working as the grape boycott organizer, Marion Moses also ran the farmworkers' clinic and worked as a nurse. Since she had started working at the clinic several years before, she had repeatedly seen women whose health had been compromised by a lack of access to birth control. Whether they wanted to or not, many women got pregnant year after year, giving birth to children they could not afford to feed and allowing the frequent pregnancies to weaken their bodies and tax their spirits.

For years, Moses, a practicing Roman Catholic, had supported

Church teachings about contraception and abortion, but her experiences as a nurse forced her to question these positions. The families under her care suffered from malnutrition, infant and maternal mortality, and mental-health challenges caused by too many pregnancies. She prayerfully considered her options and decided as a matter of conscience that she would provide information about birth control to women who were interested.

Moses then went one step further. A diabetic mother of seven children begged Moses for help getting birth control pills. The woman, who also suffered from high blood pressure, realized that another pregnancy could kill her. What would happen to her children then? Moses found a doctor willing to prescribe birth control pills, and she carefully monitored the woman's health every month. Moses and her patient kept the prescription a secret between them.

Eventually, the woman's husband found out that she was taking contraceptives. Enraged, he complained to Chavez, who agreed with the husband and told Moses she could never provide birth control to the women at the clinic again.

Moses stood by her medical decision. She told Chavez that he could either trust her to use her best medical judgment or he could find another nurse willing to work for the low wages she was offered at the clinic. He backed down, and she stayed for several more years. When Moses left the clinic, she didn't give up in defeat: At age thirty-six, she decided to go to medical school to become a doctor.

Steinem supported Moses and agreed with her decision to offer birth control information. Steinem felt frustrated by the sexism and discrimination women experienced both in the farm-worker community and in her own life as a young woman in New York City, but she wasn't sure what to do about it. She encountered daily injustices and outright prejudice—limited work opportunities, lower wages, belittling comments—but sexism was accepted as the way the world worked. Steinem had heard about the women's movement, but she didn't think it had much to do with her. She was not yet a feminist, but that was about to change.

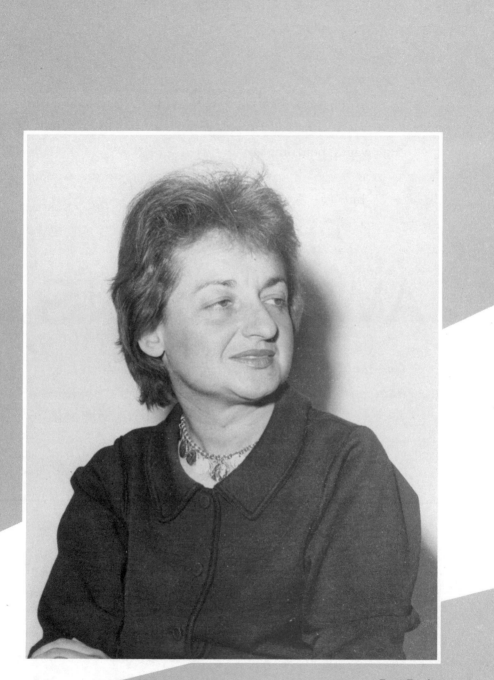

Betty Friedan
[Library of Congress]

CHAPTER 15

FEMINIST AWAKENING

Once the light began to dawn, I couldn't understand why I hadn't figured out any of this before.

—GLORIA STEINEM

Like millions of other women, Gloria Steinem had read the 1963 bestseller *The Feminine Mystique* by Betty Friedan. She sympathized with the struggles facing the suburban housewives depicted in the book, but, frankly, she didn't see what the women's movement had to do with her. Steinem was a single working woman living in New York City. She had to put up with job discrimination, lower wages than her male colleagues, and sexual harassment at work, but wasn't that just the way things were?

In *The Feminine Mystique*, Friedan reported the results of a survey she had taken of her Smith College classmates for their fifteenth reunion. Friedan found that most of the women who responded felt unfulfilled in their roles as housewives and mothers; they resented being trapped and stifled by their traditional domestic responsibilities. She argued that modern American women were defined through their service relationships—as "husband's wife, children's mother, server of physical needs of husband, children, home"—and not as separate individuals with their own interests and desires and passions. These ideas may seem self-evident today, but they were revolutionary in their time.

The book became a bestseller and ignited the modern women's movement, turning millions of women into feminists. Women began to rethink their role in society, challenging rather than passively accepting their traditional expectations.

Steinem didn't identify with "the feminine mystique" because she had already defied many cultural expectations. She wasn't a wife or a mother. She didn't live in the suburbs or depend on a man for financial support. She thought the women's movement belonged to white, well-educated, middle-class, unemployed suburban women. It wasn't her battle.

"I shared the reaction [to feminism] of many working-class women and women of color," Steinem later wrote. She supported women getting out of their homes and working if that's what they wanted to do, but she was already in the workforce struggling to get by. "The women's movement isn't for me," she concluded. Instead of working on women's liberation, Steinem continued to focus her efforts on ending the war in Vietnam, promoting the struggles of farmworkers, and fighting for civil rights for African Americans.

Publication of *The Feminine Mystique* marked the beginning of what became known as the second wave of feminism. The first wave had been a nineteenth-century movement that began in 1848 when early feminists met in Seneca Falls, New York, and held the first American convention supporting women's rights. Their efforts soon focused on women's suffrage—the right to vote—an issue that was not resolved until 1920 when the Nineteenth Amendment to the Constitution was finally passed by Congress and ratified by three-fourths of the states. Friedan's work reignited the women's movement.

In 1966, the women's movement became more political when Betty Friedan and twenty-eight other feminists organized the National Organization for Women (NOW), a group dedicated to transforming feminist fury into political and legal change. NOW worked on equal legal rights, equal opportunities in education and employment, reproductive freedom, and increased female partic-ipation in the political system. While Steinem supported NOW's agenda, she didn't think the group did enough to address the needs of low-income women, lesbians, and women of color. She believed the women's movement should also embrace younger and more rad-ical feminists. Steinem agreed with the mission, but she didn't iden-tify strongly enough to become a feminist missionary at that time.

A more radical branch of feminists was also taking shape. This group made headlines in 1968 during a demonstration at the Miss

America pageant. About two hundred women gathered outside the hotel where the beauty contest was taking place; they marched, carried posters, and crowned a live sheep the true Miss America. As part of their protest, they filled a garbage can with objects they associated with female oppression, including dish towels, false eyelashes, girdles, steno pads, *Playboy* and *Cosmopolitan* magazines, and, famously, brassieres. The media and public fixated on the undergarments, and the pejorative term *bra burner* was born. (It should be noted that the protesters never lit a fire or burned anything because they didn't have the necessary permit to start a fire. They were feminists, not arsonists.) Steinem found these feisty feminists engaging, but she still wasn't ready to claim the movement as her own.

· · · · · · · ·

STEINEM MAY NOT have been interested in NOW, but NOW was interested in her. In December 1968, Steinem appeared on a television program with Jean Faust, the national legislative chairperson of NOW. Faust was impressed with Steinem, and after the show the two women went out for coffee. Faust encouraged Steinem to get involved with NOW, but Steinem politely declined, explaining that she considered herself a *humanist* rather than a *feminist*.

A few weeks later, Faust approached Steinem again, this time asking her to join a group of women who were planning a demonstration outside the Oak Room, a restaurant at the Plaza Hotel that refused to serve women during lunch. Steinem agreed to cover the protest as a reporter and possibly write about it in her City Politic column for *New York* magazine, but she didn't want to be directly affiliated with the group.

The story appealed to Steinem because she was already irked at the staff of the Plaza Hotel. She had recently been there to conduct an interview over tea in the Palm Court restaurant. She had arrived early and waited in the lobby. After a few minutes, the hotel manager told her that "unescorted ladies" were not allowed to stand in the lobby. Steinem explained that she was waiting for a guest, but the manager insisted that she had to leave. "I was humiliated," Steinem said. "Did I look like a prostitute?"

Several weeks later, the same scene played out again. Steinem scheduled another interview at the Plaza, but this time she tried to avoid the drama by arranging to do the interview in the guest's suite. When she saw the manager, she decided to take a minute to see if he would approach her again. "Sure enough, the manager approached me with his same officious speech," Steinem said. "But this time I was amazed to hear myself saying some very different things." Instead of backing down, Steinem pushed back. She told the manager it was a public lobby and she had a legal right to stand there. She asked him why he hadn't chased away the "unescorted men," suggesting that they might be male prostitutes.

Startled, the manager left her alone. Instead of conducting her interview upstairs, Steinem changed her plans. "I called my subject and suggested we have tea downstairs after all," she said.

Later, Steinem thought about what had changed between her first and second encounter with the manager. "When I faced the hotel manager again, I had glimpsed the world *as if women mattered*," Steinem said. "By seeing through their eyes, I had begun to see through my own."

In the late 1960s, Steinem was writing more frequently about the women's movement, and some of the ideas were resonating with her. "Feminist ideas began to explode," she said. Steinem began to realize that women were judged on how they looked, rather than what was in their heads and hearts. Too many women didn't feel they could go to the grocery store without lipstick; they gave more thought to what they wore than what they read. Steinem had had enough. "I abandoned clothes anxiety with relief and evolved a simple, comfortable, jeans-sweater-and-boots uniform that I wore for one entire decade," she said.

Steinem experienced sexism and discrimination on a regular basis, but—like most women—she accepted the status quo because she didn't think she could change it. Once she began to see the world through a feminist lens, she was no longer willing to tolerate things the way they stood. She was on her way to embracing feminism, but her real moment of transformation occurred a few months later when she began to research a story for her City Politic column in *New York* magazine.

• • • • • • • •

THE FLYER READ: "Abortion: Women Tell It Like It Is," a presentation of the Redstockings, the women's liberation movement, at Washington Square Methodist Church. The meeting was intended to be a feminist response to a hearing on abortion that had been held by the New York State legislature. In the official proceedings, the lawmakers had accepted testimony from fourteen "experts" on abortion: thirteen male doctors, lawyers, and clergymen, and one woman—a Catholic nun. They had refused to hear from women who had actual experience with abortion.

Steinem was curious about what the women had to say. On March 21, 1969, she went to the church and settled in at the back of the crowded room. The meeting opened with a speaker who acknowledged the bravery of the women who planned to speak. At the time, abortion was illegal in the United States, so the speakers were not only sharing intimate details of their personal lives, but also admitting to breaking the law.

One by one, twelve women—"the real experts"—spoke about their experiences with abortion.

"You get into a car at Fifty-Fourth Street and Lexington Avenue and you're blindfolded and taken someplace, you don't know where."

"You're not given an anesthetic. The instruments aren't even sterilized."

"I went to eleven hospitals before one would give me an abortion. The doctors at the tenth offered me a deal: I could have an abortion if I agreed to be sterilized. I was twenty."

Steinem had expected to cover the meeting as a reporter, objectively recording the events and writing a thoughtful and balanced story, but memories of her own pregnancy overwhelmed her. She had assumed that her abortion no longer affected her—it was part of the past, no longer relevant to who she was today—but that night her feelings were just as raw and real as they had been years before, when she was a twenty-two-year-old student in London, alone, afraid, and willing to do almost anything to end her pregnancy.

That night Steinem experienced an epiphany that she later described as "the great blinding light bulb" that suddenly illuminated a previously dark room. The women spoke about their personal experiences, trusting those who were listening to respond with compassion and to realize that they were not alone. Steinem had never before heard people speak so openly and honestly about their lives.

Steinem knew that she had been lucky to have had a safe and legal abortion while in London, rather than to have tried to end her pregnancy in the United States. "I had had an abortion, too, but I'd been lucky enough to be in England, where laws were slightly less punishing," Steinem wrote. "I never forgot the weeks of panic before I found a doctor, or how it had changed my life . . . yet I'd never spoken to anyone about this major experience in my life." For the first time, Steinem began to question the system that criminalized female reproductive choice. "I began to wonder *why* it was illegal; *why* our reproductive lives are not under our own control and *why* this fundamental issue hadn't been part of any other social justice movement," she wrote.

When it came time to write her article, Steinem held back. "I researched as much as I could about reproductive issues and other wellsprings of new feminism and wrote a respectable, objective article," Steinem said. Her article, "After Black Power, Women's Liberation," was a thoughtful and intellectually provocative article, but it didn't reveal Steinem's heart. "It contained none of the emotions I had felt in that church basement, and certainly not the fact that I, too, had an abortion," she wrote.

Steinem said she became a feminist that night. This was the first consciously feminist article she wrote. In it, Steinem explored the natural overlap of the civil rights and women's rights movements.

She encouraged the intersection of the movements, noting that if they supported each other, both would be more likely to succeed and "a long-lasting and important mass movement would result." The thought-provoking article won the Penney-Missouri Journalism Award in 1970.

When Steinem left the meeting, she began to study feminist theory. She developed a deeper appreciation for her own childhood, and for the first time she began to see her mother's mental illness in part as a consequence of a woman forced by society to neglect her personal ambition as a writer to meet the needs of her family. Feminism had everything to do with her. Steinem understood that she had rebelled against marriage and motherhood because she had devoted so much of her childhood to taking care of her mother's needs.

Steinem reinterpreted many things she had taken for granted in her own life. She said she had to learn to trust her own experience. "It is truly amazing how long we can go on accepting myths that oppose our own lives, assuming instead that we are the odd exceptions," she said. "But once the light began to dawn, I couldn't understand why I hadn't figured out any of this before."

From that point forward, Steinem looked at the world through the lens of feminism. She saw gender as a caste system no less oppressive than the caste system she had fought against in India years before. She had gone to the speak-out on abortion hoping to find a good story, and she had an experience that changed the direction of her life.

Gloria with Dorothy Pitman Hughes

[Dan Wynn]

CHAPTER 16

FINDING HER VOICE

I would have remained silent . . . if I hadn't been lucky enough to enter a time when a few women were beginning to figure out that our gigantic lack of confidence wasn't all due to our individual faults.

— GLORIA STEINEM

By 1970, the second wave of feminism had washed over the entire United States. Major stories about the women's movement appeared in *Time*, *Newsweek*, *Atlantic Monthly*, *New York Times Magazine*, *U.S. News & World Report*, *Esquire*, and *Saturday Review*, among other publications. For the most part, these articles reported a fairly bleak economic picture for women:

Male high school graduates earned more than female college graduates; one-third of women worked outside the home, but they earned only 58 percent of what men were paid for the same work. *Time* described women's status "as relentlessly second class as . . . any minority."

While doing research for some of these articles, a number of female journalists learned about the unfair conditions in their own places of employment. In March 1970, forty-six women at *Newsweek* magazine filed a complaint with the Equal Employment Opportunity Commission, charging discrimination against women in hiring and promotion as well as pay. At the time, *Newsweek* hired men to be writers and women to be researchers.

The same month, about two hundred women from three feminist groups—NOW, the Redstockings, and the New York Radical Feminists—stormed the offices of *Ladies' Home Journal*, demanding that the magazine stop publishing articles that were "irrelevant, unstimulating, and demeaning to the women of America." Instead, they wanted the magazine to cover reproductive health, childcare, and other issues of importance to women. After an eleven-hour standoff, the editors agreed to write a special issue covering the topics the women wanted.

In this period of rising female consciousness, Gloria Steinem found a much more receptive audience when she pitched feminist story ideas to editors. To mark the fiftieth anniversary of female suffrage, Steinem wrote an essay for *Time* titled "What It Would Be Like If Women Win." In the article she reassured readers that feminists did not plan to turn women into men. "Any change is fearful, especially one affecting both politics and sex roles," she wrote. But feminism was not to be feared, she explained. "Women don't want to exchange places with men. . . . That is not our goal."

Steinem argued that feminism offered nothing more—and nothing less—than equal opportunity for both men and women. "We do want to change the economic system to one more based on merit," she wrote. Instead of reversing roles, Steinem favored a world where both women and men "will be free to choose according to individual talents and preferences." (Steinem did not know at the time that *Time* magazine paid less for her essay than it paid for essays written by male authors.)

As Steinem wrote more frequently about women's issues, she began to get pushback from male writers and editors who asked her why she was wasting time writing about women's issues instead of taking on *real assignments*. She had fought to earn respect as a writer, and now she was giving up her chance to cover *important* topics.

Steinem might have questioned her choices a few years earlier, but she had grown in her understanding of feminism to the point that she recognized that the question itself was part of the problem. The marginalization of women's issues was proof of the marginalization of women themselves. Steinem knew that she could speak out as a feminist, but she would have a price to pay in terms of her career. Again, many male editors refused to take her seriously.

"There seems to be no punishment inside the white male club that quite equals the ridicule and personal viciousness reserved for women who rebel," she said. Steinem said she felt she was treated like "a dirty joke." Despite the cost to her career, Steinem chose to be a female rebel rather than join the male establishment. She then learned to use her voice, both as a writer and a speaker.

SEVERAL MONTHS AFTER she wrote about feminism in her *New York* magazine column, Steinem was asked to address the Women's National Democratic Club about her prizewinning article. She was interested in—but terrified about—speaking publicly.

"The very idea of speaking to a group, much less before a big audience, was enough to make my heart pound and my mouth go dry," she said. "The few times I tried it, I became obsessed with whether or not I could get to the end of each sentence without swallowing, and then obsessed for days afterward with what I could and should have said."

She had experienced this terror before. In her capacity as a writer, she had sometimes been asked to appear on radio and television programs to discuss her work. She had earned a negative reputation for backing out of speaking engagements at the last minute. "In the past when magazines had booked me on a radio or television show . . . I had canceled out at the last minute so often that a few shows banned me as a guest," she said. Steinem wasn't afraid of talking to anyone when she was acting as a journalist, but she struggled to get over her self-consciousness as a public speaker.

In an attempt to overcome her fear, Steinem consulted a speech teacher who told her that writers and dancers tend to have trouble with public speaking because they have chosen professions in which they communicate without spoken words. Steinem noted that she had danced throughout her childhood before becoming a writer. Addressing an audience did not come naturally to her.

"I would have remained silent, like so many women who were

giving up on various aspects of our human abilities, if I hadn't been lucky enough to enter a time when a few women were beginning to figure out that our gigantic lack of confidence wasn't all due to our individual faults," Steinem wrote. "There was a profound system of sexual politics at work here." She realized her anxiety stemmed from a fear of judgment: "It's a problem that seems to be common among people who feel overly dependent on the approval of others."

Steinem became more comfortable with public speaking by sharing the stage with other women. A few months before she was asked to speak at the Women's National Democratic Club, Steinem wrote an article about day care for *New York* magazine. As part of her research, she had interviewed Dorothy Pitman Hughes, a woman who had started a childcare center in an abandoned storefront on New York's Upper West Side. The two women hit it off: During the interview, they got into a conversation with one of Hughes's coworkers, who didn't want his future wife to work after they married. Steinem and Hughes challenged his assumptions about marriage, and, in the end, he had a more open-minded view of women's right to work. That conversation showed a similarity in thinking and a personal chemistry that convinced Steinem that she and Hughes could make a great speaking duo.

In the end, Steinem accepted the invitation to speak at the Women's National Democratic Club, with the understanding that she copresent with Hughes, who had years of experience speaking to church groups, neighborhood associations, and civil rights organizations. Steinem admired the fact that Hughes got things done: She had started the childcare center because she needed it. She sang in clubs at night, but she needed childcare help so that she could have a chance to sleep and rehearse during the days. When she applied for day care, she was told she had to go on welfare or claim that her husband beat her. She refused and opened what became the West 80th Street Day Care Center, a multiethnic cooperative that provided job training for women as well as childcare.

Hughes put Steinem at ease on the stage, but her presence also changed the message: Having an African American speaking partner showed that the women's movement belonged to all women, regardless of their race, age, or income. Steinem wanted to represent an inclusive and progressive version of feminism. "Right away we discovered that a white woman and a Black woman speaking together attracted far more diverse audiences than either one of us would have done on our own," Steinem said.

After the speech, a representative from a speakers' bureau asked Steinem if she would be willing to speak about feminism on college campuses and in community centers nationwide. Again, she agreed, if Hughes could join her. (Even though Steinem was better known, she always split the speaker's fee evenly with anyone who presented with her.) Steinem spoke first—she knew that her presentation would seem dry and flat if she were to follow Hughes.

The feminist twosome took off, and Steinem began a career as a public speaker that would extend for decades. When Hughes had another baby, Steinem encouraged her to bring the infant along. "She would nurse the baby while I spoke, and I would hold the baby while she spoke," Steinem said. "I'm sure there were people in the audience who thought we had this baby together."

The following year, Hughes had a third child, so she cut back on the number of speeches she wanted to give. Rather than going solo, Steinem partnered with Florynce "Flo" Kennedy, the lawyer, activist, and author of *Abortion Rap* (with Diane Schulder), *Color Me Flo: My Hard Life and Good Times*, and *Sex Discrimination in Employment: An Analysis and Guide for Practitioner and Student* (with William F. Pepper).

Kennedy was a charismatic and flamboyant character, known for her cowboy hats and pink sunglasses, as well as her ruthless tongue and unfiltered wit. Kennedy was unapologetically herself. She had enrolled as a prelaw student at Columbia night school when she was twenty-eight. She earned top grades, but when she applied to law school, she was rejected. She visited the dean and told him, "If you have admitted any white man with lower grades than mine, then I want to get in, too." Fearing a discrimination lawsuit, they let her in. Kennedy graduated from Columbia Law School in 1951 and went into private practice, handling matrimonial work and some criminal cases.

As a speaking partner, Kennedy was bold and outrageous, and she encouraged Steinem—who she called "Glo-ball"—to relax and be outrageous, too. "It was Flo especially who taught me that a revolution without humor is as hopeless as one without music," Steinem wrote.

Steinem was with Kennedy in a taxi on the way to the Boston airport and they were discussing abortion. The driver, an old Irish woman, turned around at a traffic light and said, "Honey, if men could get pregnant, abortion would be a sacrament!" Steinem quoted the taxi driver so often that the phrase became an iconic feminist expression.

Kennedy spiced up Steinem's style. "Flo also rescued me from a habit that might have been okay in articles but was death in speeches: citing a lot of facts and statistics," Steinem said. After she gave a particularly heavy speech, one weighed down with facts and statistics, Kennedy gave her some tough-love feedback. "Look, if you're lying in a ditch with a truck on your ankle, you don't send somebody to the library to find out how much the truck weighs. You get it *off*," she said. Steinem took the message to heart and began to change the tone of her remarks, drawing in her audience with anecdotes and stories rather than inundating them with numbers.

Steinem became a compelling speaker who introduced generations of women to the idea of feminism, which she defined as "the equality and full humanity of women and men," a definition that appealed to a wide range of people because it didn't put one group in conflict with the other.

At the end of every presentation, Steinem and her copresenters left time for questions and answers. She wanted to know what the audience was thinking and what changes they wanted to see in their community. During the discussion, people often asked if she was a lesbian and commented on Steinem's appearance. She was used to it—much was often made of her long, manicured fingernails and blond-streaked long hair—but Steinem wanted to remind the audience to focus on the message and not the messenger. She came up with a certain response that she used repeatedly: "Nobody ever talks about Ralph Nader's looks [or about his romances or marital status], so why are you asking about mine?" She didn't want to scold the audience, but she did want to remind them not to judge her based on how she looked.

People often asked Steinem about her sexuality. At one event, an aggressive man in the audience accused Steinem and Kennedy of being lesbians. Kennedy shut him down, looking him over and saying, "Are you my alternative?" Most of the time, Steinem simply responded, "Thank you." "It disclosed nothing, confused the accuser, conveyed solidarity with women who were lesbians, and made the audience laugh," Steinem said.

When Kennedy could no longer join Steinem on the road due to health problems, she introduced Steinem to Margaret Sloan-Hunter, a Black feminist who had recently come out as a lesbian. Sloan-Hunter was in her twenties, so she brought a more youthful voice to the cause. She later became a writer at *Ms.* magazine. All three of Steinem's speaking partners were African American, and their voices helped Steinem attract audiences beyond the white, upper-middle-class women who dominated the movement. Steinem and each of her speaking partners offered up an inclusive, hopeful vision of what feminism could be. Steinem recognized feminism as an issue relevant to women of color, and she favored bringing women of all races into the movement so that they could speak for themselves.

On the lecture circuit, Steinem became a feminist prophet, spreading the word across the country, from campus to campus, woman to woman. "Though we tried to focus on parts of the country that were most removed from the little feminist activity that then existed, there were so few feminist speakers that we ended up going to almost every kind of community and, I think, every state but Alaska," she wrote.

Steinem became a major voice of the women's movement.

In time, she overcame most—but not all—of her fear of public speaking. "Years of getting up in front of audiences have taught me only three lessons: 1) you don't die; 2) there's no right way to speak, only *your* way; and 3) it's worth it," Steinem wrote.

During her career, Steinem published more than a half dozen books and hundreds of articles, but she still found a special energy in conversation. "A mutual understanding comes from being together in a room," she said. Magic happens in a give-and-take conversation in a way that can't in a one-way message on a printed page. Steinem had mastered her voice, and she had a lot to say.

Gloria Steinem at a news conference for the
Women's Action Alliance. January 1972
[Warren K. Leffler/Library of Congress]

CHAPTER 17

FEMINIST FEUD

The media tried to make her a celebrity, but no one should mistake her for a leader.

— BETTY FRIEDAN

Not everyone was interested in what Gloria Steinem had to say about the women's movement. Before Steinem came along, Betty Friedan had been the unofficial feminist spokeswoman, the one reporters turned to when they needed a quote or a comment for a story about feminism or women's liberation. But once Steinem started to speak about women's rights, reporters couldn't get enough of her. She had it all: She was articulate, witty, photogenic, and she knew how to give the interviewers just the anecdote or punch line they needed for their stories.

Steinem and Friedan did not always see eye to eye on issues of concern to women. For example, Steinem supported lesbian rights and thought issues of gender identity and discrimination should be addressed by the women's movement. Friedan did not.

Friedan wanted feminist lesbians kept in the shadows; after all, the women's movement had enough resistance without taking on homosexuality as well. Friedan argued that women should be free to love whoever they wish in private, but combining feminism and lesbian rights would alienate heterosexual women who were afraid of being labeled as lesbians. Friedan called the issue the "lavender menace" and complained that a group of lesbians were conspiring to take over the leadership of NOW.

Steinem advocated for gay rights as human rights. Rather than silence lesbians in fear of possible prejudice, she favored defending homosexuals with courage and confidence in order to help them overcome bigotry. The issue of lesbians in the women's movement had first surfaced in 1967 when writer Rita Mae Brown joined NOW and began to try to educate straight women about the unique challenges faced by lesbians, who had to deal with the double discrimination of being both female and homosexual.

The debate within the women's movement went public in December 1970 when *Time* magazine reported that well-known feminist Kate Millett was bisexual. "Kate Millett herself contributed to the growing skepticism about the movement by acknowledging at a recent meeting that she is bisexual," the editors said in an article titled "Women's Lib: A Second Look." Instead of dismissing her sexuality as irrelevant to her activism, the magazine bought into the idea that an individual's sexual orientation could invalidate their political opinions. "The disclosure is bound to discredit her as a spokeswoman for her cause, cast further doubt on her theories, and reinforce the views of those skeptics who routinely dismiss all liberationists as lesbians," the magazine editors wrote.

Instead of backing down, Steinem and a group of about fifty feminists held a "Kate Is Great" press conference. Millett read a statement describing the shared goals of the women's liberation and homosexual rights movements. Both groups wanted "a society free from defining and categorizing people by virtue of gender and/or sexual preference," Millet said. "'Lesbian' is a label used as a psychic weapon to keep women locked into their male-defined 'feminine role.' The essence of that role is that a woman is defined in terms of her relationships to men."

Steinem sat next to Millett during the press conference, holding her hand. Steinem's relationships with men had been publicized in the press, but reporters still asked if she was a lesbian; Steinem refused to answer because she didn't want to distance herself from the people she was advocating for. In future discussions, Steinem pointed out that the issue of lesbianism was another example of how society demanded that women conform to male expectations of female sexuality.

Years later, Steinem admitted that she had never had a sexual relationship with a woman. "Monosexual," she said. "It sounds so boring." Steinem said she believes that most people are bisexual and then socialized to meet cultural norms and expectations. "It's wonderful now to see young women and some young men, too, who really do fall in love with the person, not the sex," Steinem said.

· · · · · · · ·

STEINEM WASN'T ONLY emerging as a feminist spokeswoman, she was also becoming part of the story herself. In the early 1970s, *Vogue*, *Life*, *Redbook*, *Esquire*, and *Newsweek* published articles about Steinem as a feminist. In August 1971, *Newsweek* featured Steinem on its cover for a special report titled "The New Woman." Steinem had refused to pose for a cover photo because she didn't want to become the face of the movement; she knew the movement was much greater than any single figure. To get around Steinem's request, a *Newsweek* photographer shot the picture secretly through a telephoto lens during a welfare rights rally.

McCall's editors named Steinem the 1972 Woman of the Year and the "most effective spokeswoman and symbol" of the women's movement. "She is, in short, a transitional figure, proof that change is not so frightening after all, and that it has to come—for the good of women and men alike," the magazine editors wrote.

Steinem made feminism look fun. She had an exciting life as a writer; she dated rich, famous, and attractive men; and she traveled across the country to be cheered by adoring crowds. Reporters often described Steinem as "the pretty one," which always made her uncomfortable. The comment perpetuated the myth that most feminists weren't attractive enough to get a man. "This was especially clear to me because I was judged much prettier *after*

I was identified as a feminist than I ever had been *before*," she said. She resented that the comment objectified her and evaluated her based on her beauty and attractiveness to men. It wasn't a compliment; it was proof of why feminism was necessary and important.

It wasn't long before reporters turned on her. The media placed Steinem on a pedestal as the smart and attractive feminist icon, only so that they could knock her down. *Esquire* magazine published a hurtful profile of Steinem titled "SHE." The article, written by Leonard Levitt, depicted her as "the intellectuals' pinup," a shrewd and wily woman who manipulated men to get ahead in her career. "This woman, who advanced in public favor by appealing to powerful men, has moved to the front ranks of women's liberation, appealing now to women who do not like powerful men," Levitt wrote.

This vicious portrayal offended Steinem, who wasn't used to such cruel remarks. It took time and distance for her to realize that she was being criticized because she was successful. Steinem and the ideas she represented threatened the patriarchy, or the social system that kept men in positions of power and authority. Steinem enjoyed cultural and social privileges that contributed to her success—she was young, attractive, white, intelligent, and socially well connected—but she devoted a great deal of effort to promoting the equality of all people, regardless of race, class, or sexual orientation.

Because Steinem got so much attention, some feminists resented her and considered her an opportunist. Some of them had spent years working in the women's movement, only to have Steinem step in and appear to take credit for their ideas. "I often grew cross as I saw hard-won, original insights developed by others in near total anonymity be turned by the media into Gloria Steinem pronouncements, Gloria Steinem ideas, and Gloria Steinem visions," said activist and author Susan Brownmiller.

Steinem's most outspoken feminist critic was Betty Friedan. Friedan, who was known as the "Mother Superior of Women's Lib," prized her status in the movement. The middle-aged, divorced mother of three had once been America's best-known feminist—after all, she was the author of *The Feminine Mystique*, the bestselling book that had started it all—and she wasn't going to sit quietly and allow Steinem to take her place.

Friedan had legitimate political differences of opinion with Steinem, coupled with old-fashioned, run-of-the-mill jealousy. It was one thing for Steinem to be quoted in newspapers and magazines, but Friedan became enraged when Steinem was asked to be the speaker at Smith College's commencement. Friedan had never been invited back to address her alma mater to speak on graduation day, and she desperately wanted to do so.

Steinem's Smith speech turned out to be a fiasco. Steinem wrote and rewrote the speech, which she titled "The Politics of Women," right up until she took her place at the podium. She began by telling the audience how strange it was to be back at college. She said she would have expected the university to choose a man, probably old and definitely white.

She didn't offer the kind of wisdom most people expected to hear at a graduation speech. "Let me say to you some of the things that I wish so desperately someone had said to me," she said. Steinem said middle-class women's primary unpaid job was housework, which "is after all the only work that is only noticed if you don't do it. It is the definition of women's work, which is shit work." She characterized the illegality of abortion as "the number one health problem among women." She made her point about job discrimination by quoting Flo Kennedy that "there are only a few jobs that actually require a penis or vagina." Steinem's often crass remarks offended many refined parents and grandparents, even if they were well received by most of the graduates. In hindsight, she said that she wished she had taken more time to tailor her remarks for the occasion. After all, she was speaking at a college graduation, not a consciousness-raising meeting.

Friedan never would have made a speech like Steinem's.

Both Steinem and Friedan wanted the same goal—female equality—but they went about trying to achieve it in very different ways. Friedan was a reformer; Steinem was a revolutionary. Friedan talked about discrimination; Steinem talked about systemic oppression. Friedan wanted more economic opportunities for women; Steinem wanted to replace the patriarchal, male-centered family structure and the capitalist economic system, which depended on unpaid female domestic labor.

These differences became striking in the ways the two feminists spoke about marriage. Friedan identified "the problem that has no name"—female dissatisfaction with their lives as wives and mothers—but Steinem challenged the institution of marriage itself. She called the traditional father-centered nuclear family "a five- or ten-thousand-year-old experiment that we should just declare a failure." She said, "The women's movement is not the cause of divorce, marriage is."

Instead of focusing on conventional marriage as the only way to define a family, Steinem argued that the two-parent, male-female family was just one option among many different ways to structure a family. She also recognized that many women would be better off if they opted out of traditional marriage. "With homemakers having the highest rate of alcoholism, chemical dependency, and depression, the most dangerous place for a woman is in her home," Steinem said.

Friedan had no patience for such radical talk. She sometimes resorted to name-calling, describing Steinem and other radical feminists as "female chauvinist boors," playing with the feminist expression "male chauvinist pigs." When referring to Steinem's efforts to support the farmworkers' union, Friedan called her rival "the princess among the grape pickers."

At other times, Friedan tried to undermine Steinem by attacking her role in the women's movement itself. In a speech at Trinity College in 1972, Friedan argued that Steinem had "never been part of the organized" women's liberation movement because she was not a member of NOW. She told a reporter at *Newsweek*: "Gloria has not advanced any new ideas in the women's movement—but she's an outstanding publicist."

Friedan acknowledged Steinem's popularity but not her power within the movement. "The media tried to make her a celebrity, but no one should mistake her for a leader," Friedan said.

Steinem typically ignored the insults because she didn't want to give ammunition to reporters who were eager to portray the women's movement as a group of squabbling women in a catfight. "I never responded in person or print on the grounds that it would only feed the stereotype that women couldn't get along," Steinem said. The result was that Friedan wasn't held accountable, so she continued to attack.

Friedan hit a nerve when she charged Steinem with "ripping off the movement for profit" during a question-and-answer session after a lecture. In response, Steinem fired back. "The truth is that [working in the women's movement] continues to cost me money," Steinem said. "And every penny is worth it."

Instead of apologizing, Friedan insisted that she was quoted out of context. To the media, she said, there was "no feud between Gloria and me."

After years of being attacked, Steinem tried to lower her public profile. By the end of 1974, she was quoted in *People* magazine as saying she was tired of people writing about her. At that point, she had cut the number of her public appearances from fifteen a month to five. She came up with a guiding principle: "Don't do anything that another feminist could do instead."

Steinem was growing weary personally, but she also realized that a broader base of leadership would strengthen the women's movement. "It's the practice of the media to set up leaders and knock them down, which is very damaging to movements," she said. "We need to have enough women in the public eye so that we can't all be knocked down." Steinem knew the women's movement was stronger than any single person.

Gwendolyn Sawyer Cherry, first Black woman legislator in
Florida, and Congresswoman Shirley Chisholm at the Democratic
National Convention in Miami Beach, 1972
[Wikimedia Commons]

CHAPTER 18

THE
NATIONAL WOMEN'S
POLITICAL CAUCUS

At that Democratic Convention held in July in Miami, political women were in the national spotlight for the first time since suffrage.
— GLORIA STEINEM

Gloria Steinem and Betty Friedan may have had their differences, but they both knew they couldn't allow their bickering to interfere with their work. One mission that they both supported was the creation of a national political coalition that would advocate for women's rights and the election of female candidates. It was clear to Steinem and other feminist leaders that women needed to have more representation in local and national government. In 1971, there were *no* female Supreme Court justices or state governors; there was only *one* woman serving in the US Senate and only *twelve* in the US House of Representatives.

If women wanted to change the laws, they needed to become the lawmakers. Women deserved representation in government, and they began to realize that no one was going to give them that power. They were going to have to claim it for themselves. In response, in 1971, Steinem, Friedan, Congresswoman Bella Abzug, Congresswoman Shirley Chisholm (the first Black woman elected to the US House of Representatives), and a number of other women founded the National Women's Political Caucus (NWPC).

The group represented Democrats and Republicans, rich and poor, radicals and reformers, whites and women of color. With such a diverse constituency, the women realized that to make change they had to make compromises. They had frequent disagreements, but whenever possible, they tried to find common ground.

From its inception, the NWPC wanted to make a difference in the 1972 elections. To do that, they needed to get organized quickly. Steinem helped to research the names of several hundred women who were invited to the founding meeting. She looked for prospective members at feminist groups, the YWCA, the National Council of Negro Women, and the National Council of Jewish Women, among other organizations.

The first challenge was to figure out the group's mission. Friedan favored a broad-based, bipartisan approach; she thought the NWPC should support all female candidates, regardless of their positions on key issues. Bella Abzug thought the group should represent a clear ideology and should support candidates based on their positions on women's issues, rather than their sex. "I feel our obligation is to build a real political movement of women for social change," Abzug said. "Do we want the kind of women who are going to vote for missiles and Vietnam wars?"

Abzug also favored diversity. She told Friedan that when choosing candidates to support she didn't want to replace "a white, male, middle-class elite with a white, female, middle-class elite." Steinem agreed. "We wanted to transform the system, not imitate it," she said.

Ultimately, it was up to the membership to decide how they wanted to structure the organization. On July 10, 1971, 320 women from twenty-six states gathered for three days in Washington, DC, to map out the course of the NWPC. They needed to answer certain fundamental questions: Should the caucus back individual candidates or simply advocate in favor of key issues? Which issues mattered most? Would the caucus support male candidates who supported women's issues?

The NWPC worked up a bold and broad mission statement, dedicating itself to "every woman whose abilities have been wasted by second-class, subservient, underpaid, or powerless positions to which female human beings are consigned. . . . To every woman who sits at home with little control over her own life, much less the powerful institutions of this country, wondering if there isn't more to life than this. . . . To every woman who has experienced the ridicule or hostility reserved by this country—and often its political leaders—for women who dare to express the hopes and ambitions that are natural to every human being."

To serve these women and carry out their vision, the NWPC decided to establish state and local caucuses. "Once chapters were established and a structure was in place, NWPC's goal was to increase the number and diversity of women delegates to both the Republican and Democratic National Conventions of 1972, and to get the Equal Rights Amendment, reproductive freedom, and other basic issues of equality written into both parties' platforms," Steinem said. To achieve those goals could have taken years, but the convention was only two months away.

The caucus universally supported a resolution against racism; the other positions supported by the group were presented as "guidelines." These guidelines included support of the Equal Rights Amendment, safe and legal access to contraception and abortion, an end to the war in Vietnam, an adequate income for all Americans, and fair treatment of workingwomen. The group pledged to organize local chapters that would encourage women to run for elected offices and assist with their campaigns; it would also pull together lists of qualified women the group would recommend for appointed positions.

As soon as the group was established, Steinem began rushing around the country to help start state and local caucuses. "Between July, when the caucus was founded, and August, when the Democratic National Convention opened in Miami, there was no time to organize women delegates and alternates state by state," Steinem said. Instead, the members came to NWPC meetings each morning for guidance. Even though they had not strategized together before, they unified and became "a force to be dealt with."

Steinem planned to attend the Democratic National Convention in Miami in 1972, but she didn't want to take on a major leadership role. In fact, she tried to avoid being assigned a top job by not attending the meeting to assign responsibilities at the convention. She was chosen to be the NWPC spokeswoman anyway. "Unfortunately, as I learned, a reluctant spokeswoman was considered more likely to represent the group, while an eager one might seek the spotlight," Steinem said. "As I was to learn, avoiding conflict causes conflict to seek you out." This was another disappointment to Friedan, who had wanted to act as spokeswoman.

Steinem had been at national political conventions before. Unlike the 1968 convention, when Steinem worked for an individual candidate, this time she focused exclusively on women's issues. She found the 1972 convention much more welcoming to women. "There was a strong women's plank in the platform, where four years ago there had been none," she said. "At that Democratic Convention held in July in Miami, political women were in the national spotlight for the first time since suffrage," Steinem said. That alone was a victory.

• • • • • • • •

ABOUT A MONTH before the convention, a core group of NWPC members met with the Democratic candidates to find out where they stood on issues of concern to women. When they met with Senator George McGovern, they pressed him about his support for legalized abortion. At one point he had supported a woman's right to choose, but he had backed down after being attacked by antiabortion groups in the primaries.

The NWPC wanted reproductive rights included in the Democratic platform. A political platform is a formal statement of the core beliefs supported by a candidate or political party. A plank is a position on an individual issue or topic within the overall platform. While a party platform isn't binding, it does reflect the key ideas and values of the party.

At the 1972 Democratic Convention, the delegates and candidates debated and carefully considered the party platform, including the issue of reproductive choice. Steinem worked to come up with a carefully worded reproductive freedom item for a political plank. It read: "The Democratic Party is opposed to government interference in the reproductive and sexual freedom of the individual American citizen."

This wasn't considered a radical position. At the time, Gallup polls showed 57 percent of Americans and 54 percent of Roman Catholics considered abortion an issue for a woman and her doctor, not government. These people didn't necessarily support abortion, they just didn't think it was the business of government to get involved.

Although the NWPC pushed for the reproductive-rights plank, a woman working on McGovern's campaign removed the issue from McGovern's draft of the platform. She said that she personally supported abortion rights, but she worried that the issue could be used against McGovern in the general election because it remained controversial. She said she did it without McGovern's knowledge.

When Steinem learned what had happened, she became so frustrated that she "wept with rage," according to those who were present.

"I cry when I get angry," Steinem said.

Although reproductive rights would not make it into the main Democratic platform, a delegate from Alaska collected enough signatures to reintroduce a version of the reproductive-rights issue as a minority plank. "The right to reproductive freedom will be raised at the convention anyway," Steinem wrote. "It's the strength of the women's movement: some of us won't be told what to do anymore, not even by each other."

The NWPC may have lost the abortion debate at the convention, but it was a breakthrough to have the issue discussed at all. "It was the first time this human right had been raised as an issue and voted on by a major party," Steinem said.

• • • • • • • •

STEINEM STUMBLED A bit when endorsing her choice for the Democratic nominee. She had initially supported Senator George McGovern, but she changed her loyalty—more or less—when New York congresswoman Shirley Chisholm joined the race in March 1972. Steinem had worked with Chisholm in the past, but she didn't think she had a chance of winning. Steinem usually had good political instincts, but this time she tried to support two candidates at once. "I'm for Shirley Chisholm—but I think that George McGovern is the best of the male candidates," she said.

Chisholm didn't care for the lukewarm endorsement. "You're supporting either George McGovern or Shirley Chisholm . . . don't do me any favors by giving me this semi-endorsement," Chisholm said. "I don't need that kind of help."

When it came time for the vote, McGovern won the nomination, but Chisholm received 151 votes in her symbolic run for women's rights, civil rights, and an end to the Vietnam War. "Shirley's mere presence in the race brought the NWPC goals to national attention," said Steinem.

In the general election, McGovern lost in a landslide to incumbent Richard Nixon; McGovern won the popular vote in only one state, Massachusetts.

After the campaign, Steinem reflected on what the NWPC involvement meant. "Women are never again going to be the mindless coffee makers in politics," she wrote. "There is no such thing as a perfect leader. We have to learn to lead ourselves." The NWPC was just getting started, but it had succeeded in part of its mission: It put women's issues on the national stage. Women had become part of the political conversation.

Phyllis Schlafly demonstrating against the Equal Rights
Amendment in front of the White House

[Library of Congress]

CHAPTER 19

THE EQUAL RIGHTS AMENDMENT

Equality of rights under the law shall not be denied or abridged by the United States or by any state on account of sex.

—THE EQUAL RIGHTS AMENDMENT

The Equal Rights Amendment (ERA) had been proposed— and defeated—by Congress every year since 1923. The amendment to the US Constitution was deceptive in its simplicity. The ERA—just twenty-four words long—read: "Equality of rights under the law shall not be denied or abridged by the United States or by any state on account of sex."

It might seem like passage of the ERA should have been a slam dunk. Didn't most Americans think that men and women should be treated equally under the law? Although the wording of the amendment is clear and straightforward, it was so broad that it left a lot of room for people to add their own fears and prejudices. Those against the ERA tried to generate fear about what equality would look like. Would the ERA end spousal support for women who divorce? Would women be forced to join the military and fight in combat? Would men and women have to use the same public bathrooms? (Concerns about bathroom use often become a distracting issue when oppressed groups seek equality.)

Steinem first weighed in on the issue in May 1970 when she testified before the US Senate in support of the amendment. "I have been denied a society in which women are encouraged, or even allowed, to think of themselves as first-class citizens and responsible human beings," Steinem testified. She noted that at the time a woman without a male escort could be refused service in a restaurant or denied the right to lease an apartment, even if the woman could afford to pay the check or cover the rent.

She raised concerns that women didn't receive equal pay for comparable work. Why should a woman who answers the phone at city hall make less than the man who answers the phone at the police precinct? Why should the "maintenance man" who works in an office during the day make more than the "maid" who works in that same office building at night? Steinem argued that women deserved the rights and responsibilities of full citizenship, including the right to equal pay for equal work.

Not everyone agreed. Conservative Phyllis Schlafly organized a group to fight against passage of the ERA. She (inaccurately) argued that the amendment would destroy families and force taxpayers to pay for abortions. She charged that the ERA would undermine states' rights, the same argument that was used against the suffragists in the nineteenth century. If the ERA simply insured equality between men and women, what rights of the states would it infringe? The right to discriminate against women? "*States' rights and local legislative control* have always been code words for racial bias and economic conservatism," Steinem said. Discrimination on the basis of sex should be considered wrong and illegal in every state.

Steinem blamed the media for allowing misinformation about the ERA to spread. "To my knowledge, not one major newspaper or radio station, not one network news department or national television show has ever done an independent investigative report on what the ERA will and will not do," Steinem said. Without specific information, people made up facts to fit their preconceived worldviews.

The debate over the ERA was further skewed by the so-called fairness doctrine in journalism, which requires that the media report both sides of an issue, balancing the time and space devoted to both sides of an argument. This doctrine made conservative Phyllis Schlafly a household name. Hers was often the voice heard in opposition to the ERA, even though she represented a minority opinion.

"In the early days of the civil rights movement, most journalists followed the same 'equal time' formula," Steinem said. For example, if a journalist covering voter registration in the South reported that civil rights workers had been beaten by the police when they were in jail, they would give equal coverage to the false claim that the organizers had beaten each other. "Readers were left with either their confusion or their original biases intact," Steinem said.

When it came to the ERA, the public heard contradictory reports. One person might argue that the ERA would strengthen the legal rights of women and create equality opportunities in the workplace, and the next person might say the amendment would eliminate child-support payments and force women to work outside the home. One person may say the ERA is a simple guarantee of democracy, while another might insist that it will destroy families, force the integration of bathrooms, and promote homosexuality. What was the public supposed to believe?

In hindsight, Steinem wishes that feminists had handled certain parts of the ERA debate differently. In the early and mid-1970s, the Vietnam War was in full swing and men eighteen and older were required by law to register for the draft. The country was divided in both its support of the war and its support of a mandatory draft. Many Americans didn't want their sons sent off to war, and they didn't want their daughters to be drafted, either.

Feminists stumbled in their handling of the draft issue. "Feminists began draft-based anti-ERA arguments with a ritual disclaimer, 'I'm opposed to the draft for men *or* women,'" Steinem said. Too often, these discussions ended with women conceding that with the ERA women would be obligated to serve in the military with men. Instead, Steinem wished that the debate had focused on the issue of choice for women and men. "The idea is not to dictate what a choice shall be, but to give each person the power to make it," Steinem said. "That means our most effective argument is the right of women to *volunteer* for the military, including combat positions, on the same basis as men." If this approach had been used, more women may have supported the ERA.

The issue of female service in the military has been a long-fought battle. During the Vietnam War and for decades afterward, women could not serve in combat roles in the military. This policy had an impact on women's military careers because high-level promotions often required combat experience. It was not until 2016 that the Department of Defense announced that women could serve in all roles—including combat—in all branches of the military, as long as they meet the requirements for a job. "The point of feminism is the power to choose," Steinem said.

. . . .

THE ERA FINALLY passed Congress on March 22, 1972, but it never became law. To change the Constitution, the amendment had to be ratified by thirty-eight states—three-fourths of the fifty United States—within seven years. That did not happen. Even though more than 60 percent of Americans supported the ERA, only thirty-five states passed the ERA by the deadline.

By the end of 1974, thirty-three states had ratified the ERA and it seemed likely that five more states would get on board. To stop that from happening, conservative forces joined together to slow the momentum. These groups included the Ku Klux Klan, the John Birch Society, conservative religious groups, Phyllis Schlafly's Stop ERA campaign and Eagle Forum, and Jerry Falwell's Moral Majority. These fear-based campaigns worked: By 1976, no additional states had ratified the ERA, and five states considered rescinding their approval.

Congress considered extending the deadline for ratification, and Katharine Graham asked Steinem to speak to the *Washington Post* editorial board about the issue. Steinem was nervous. In general, she had become more comfortable with public speaking, but this all-male editorial board made her anxious. "Speaking got easier, but there were certain kinds of audiences that could bring all the nervousness back," Steinem said. She faltered in the interview, and the editorial board came down against giving the ERA more time for ratification.

As it turned out, Congress ended up extending the deadline anyway. Still, the effort fell three states short of the necessary thirty-eight for ratification.

Instead of losing heart at the defeat, Steinem felt optimism. "One inevitable result of winning a majority change in consciousness is a backlash from those forces whose power depended on the old one," Steinem said. "Perhaps that's the first survival lesson we need to remember if we are to keep going: *serious opposition is a measure of success*. Women have been trained to measure our effectiveness in love and approval, not conflict and resistance." Another way of measuring the power of the women's movement is to measure the strength of the resistance to it. The energy of the backlash reflects the energy of the movement itself.

Ms. magazine cover, spring 1972

CHAPTER 20

PREVIEW

Ms. *is a magazine for female human beings.*

—*Ms.* MAGAZINE STATEMENT OF PURPOSE

While the nation debated the ERA, women across America organized political groups, ran for office, and discovered their voices. Women began to rethink their roles in society. It was in this pro-female period that *Ms.* magazine was first published.

The project can trace its roots back to 1969, when Harvard Law

School graduate Brenda Feigen tuned in to a late-night television program in New York City. Feigen didn't recognize the guest, a young feminist named Gloria Steinem, but she remembered seeing an "obviously intelligent, glamorous woman, thirtysomething, spouting facts and statistics about injustices of all kinds against women."

Steinem's words had a profound impact on Feigen. She had felt belittled her entire time at Harvard, starting with the opening ceremony for incoming students when the law school dean told the women in her class that they were taking the place of men who would be the breadwinners for their families. Throughout her time as a law student, Feigen felt unwelcome and alone. At the time, she took the criticism personally. Hearing Steinem speak made Feigen see her experience through feminist eyes: The discrimination she encountered wasn't personal, it was political. It wasn't about who she was, it was about the fact that she was a woman. "This was [my] first realization that what [I'd] been fighting for during those three long years in Cambridge had broader repercussions in the rest of the world," Feigen said.

After seeing Steinem on television, Feigen called the National Organization for Women's national office and asked to join them. In 1970, she was working as NOW's legislative vice president and coordinating congressional testimony in favor of the Equal Rights Amendment. She remembered Steinem and asked her if she would be willing to speak. As they worked to prepare Steinem's remarks, the two women became friends.

Feigen and Steinem cared about many of the same issues, so along with Dorothy Pitman Hughes they decided to form a new organization that would help women at a local level deal with job discrimination, domestic violence, day care, and other challenges faced by women every day. Instead of talking about problems, the alliance would provide practical and meaningful support to women in need.

In 1971, they organized the Women's Action Alliance. The group became a clearinghouse for information and local resources all over the country. It also provided written materials about women's rights and how to handle common problems. In time, the alliance planned to develop information packets and other printed materials of their own.

To raise money for the alliance, Steinem and Feigen thought about starting a newsletter. "You're already too well-known to just do a newsletter," Feigen said. "We should do a magazine."

"We'll never get advertising," Steinem said.

They weren't the only ones thinking about launching a feminist magazine. At that time, there were several hundred feminist newsletters and publications, but most had very limited circulations and none were glossy national women's magazines. Another group of feminists wanted to start a magazine they planned to call *Jane*, but they couldn't get the necessary financial backing.

Steinem didn't love the idea. She had worked hard to establish her identity as a writer, and she didn't want to be pigeonholed as a feminist writer. She thrived in the unpredictable world of freelance writing and didn't want to get tied down to a single publication.

In January and February 1971, Steinem and Feigen invited a number of female writers and editors in New York to two meetings to discuss the idea of starting a feminist magazine. There was more than enough interest to start a publication. Feigen decided to continue to work with the Women's Action Alliance for another year, and then she left to run the American Civil Liberties Union's Women's Rights Project with Ruth Bader Ginsburg.

The three original partners in the magazine project were Steinem; Betty Harris, a public relations executive; and Patricia Carbine, the editor of *McCall's* magazine and the highest-ranking woman in magazine publishing. Carbine didn't want her name on the original masthead because she planned to continue her work at *McCall's*. In April 1971 they set up a corporation with three equal stockholders, and each of the women chipped in $126.67 for stock in a company known as Majority Enterprises. They needed to incorporate before they could raise the money they needed to get started.

Harris was supposed to bring in funds, but she wasn't success-ful. Steinem arranged to meet with Katharine Graham, owner of the *Washington Post* and *Newsweek*, who thought the idea was intriguing. She invested $20,000 of her personal money, but they were still struggling to find other investors.

At that point, Steinem received an interesting offer from Clay Felker, founder of *New York* magazine. He suggested that he pub-lish a forty-four-page sample issue of Steinem's feminist magazine as an insert in the December 1971 double issue of *New York*, as well as three hundred thousand copies of the entire 144-page preview issue for sale on newsstands. The preview issue would go on sale January 1972, but the team worried that it might sit on the news-stands for a while, so they dated it "Spring 1972." Felker's adver-tising sales staff would sell the ads to run in the magazine, and he would cover all the expenses. In exchange, he would keep the advertising money and half the profits of the newsstand sales of the three hundred thousand preview copies.

Felker's offer was fair, but it wasn't an act of charity. He thought a feminist magazine would be a moneymaker. Steinem and her partners agreed.

· · · · · · · ·

STEINEM AND THE other editors at the magazine had a clear idea of what kind of magazine they wanted to create. Instead of covering cooking and fashion, they wanted to write thought-provoking articles about politics and social reform and the legal challenges facing women. They envisioned a general-interest magazine that would cover world and national news with a feminist twist.

The magazine needed a name. The women brainstormed at a staff meeting. How about *Sisters?* Too much like a magazine for Catholic nuns. What about *Sojourner*, in honor of abolitionist and suffragist Sojourner Truth? Too much like a travel magazine.

How about *Ms.?* The title Ms. was used by some feminists who objected to a woman's title being linked to her marital status (such as Miss or Mrs.). Steinem researched the word and found that it had been used for decades by secretaries when a woman's marital status was unknown. The new magazine had a name: *Ms.* They also added a subtitle: *For a Better World*.

They came up with a statement of purpose: "*Ms.* is a magazine for female human beings. Unlike traditional women's publications, it does not identify us by role—as wives, mothers, loves or even as workers and professionals. It assumes that women are full human beings who are both complex and individual. . . . *Ms.*

will help us seize control of our own lives and humanize the values around us."

They began to polish their articles and come up with meaningful art. The cover of the preview issue featured a multitasking blue-skinned housewife-goddess with eight arms and a glowing baby growing inside her. In each hand she held a tool of the modern woman's life—an iron, a feather duster, a steering wheel, a mirror, a telephone, a clock, a frying pan, and a typewriter.

The preview issue—edited almost single-handedly by Steinem—was packed with articles that became feminist classics, including "The Housewife's Moment of Truth," "On Sisterhood," and a brave article about abortion that included a declaration "We Have Had Abortions," signed by Steinem and fifty-two other well-known women. (Steinem did not share her secret with her mother and sister until just before the article appeared.) Other useful articles included "I Want a Wife," "How to Write Your Own Marriage Contract," and "Down With Sexist Upbringing." They also included a piece about lesbians, because, Steinem said, "People said we shouldn't write about lesbians in the first issues, so naturally we had to."

The ad for *Ms.* magazine within the preview issue explained the goals of the publication. "*Ms.* is written for all women, everywhere, in every occupation and profession—women with deep, diverse ambitions, and those who have not yet had a chance to formulate ambition—women who are wives, mothers, and grandmothers, or none of these—women who want to be fully a female person and proud of it. In brief, women who want to humanize politics, business, education, the arts and sciences . . . in the home, the community, and the nation."

When the magazine was finished and sent to the printer, Steinem began a publicity tour to promote the new magazine. When she went to San Francisco in January to promote the issue, she was told that no one could find it. Steinem worried that something had gone wrong or the magazine had been shipped late. But that wasn't the issue. The newsstands were empty because all three hundred thousand copies had sold out in eight days.

Readers were ready for *Ms*.

Gloria Steinem at the offices of *Ms.* magazine
in New York City, circa 1974
[PL Gould/Getty Images]

CHAPTER 21

MS.

I remembered many, many women who said they felt "crazy" or "alone" until they found Ms. on their newsstands.

— GLORIA STEINEM

It was one thing to put out a single, preview issue and a different undertaking altogether to produce a well-crafted magazine month after month.

In the weeks following the release of the preview issue, the *Ms.* office received twenty-six thousand subscription orders and an astounding twenty thousand letters from readers. (At the time, editors expected a magazine with a circulation of about one million readers to bring in about four hundred letters in response to a typical issue.) While the initial push was inspiring, it still wasn't enough to successfully launch a magazine.

Gloria Steinem's first challenge was to convince Pat Carbine to leave *McCall's* and work at *Ms.* full-time; she did. The next issue was to replace Betty Harris, who wasn't successful at raising money and didn't get along well with the editorial staff. Steinem and Carbine negotiated a buyout; Harris got $36,000—all the money earned on the preview issue—plus she kept one-third of her stock. It was a wildly generous offer for an investment of $126.67.

A few months later, Warner Communications invested one million dollars, in exchange for 25 percent ownership of the company. With the resources needed to get the magazine off the ground, Steinem and Carbine expanded the staff and got to work.

They consciously chose to create an untraditional editorial structure. Rather than setting up the usual magazine hierarchy, they chose to eliminate titles and list staff alphabetically on the masthead, divided into the categories Editing, Publishing, and Advertising. The idea was to equally value each woman's contributions to the magazine.

"We had problems of female cultural style," Steinem said. She had a hard time taking control on the editorial side, and Pat Carbine had a hard time delegating responsibility. No one felt comfortable firing people, so the wrong people stayed on the job too long, to no one's benefit. "None of us was good at blowing her own horn," Steinem said, "which is why even now I can tell you our shortcomings more easily than our virtues."

They also tried to keep the pay structure more level than at other publications. The salaries ranged from $12,000 for a researcher to $20,000 for Steinem. "I remember we sat around a table in a Chinese restaurant and fixed each other's salaries," Steinem said. "We decided the top should be no more than three times the lowest." Steinem said she needed $15,000 a year; she was paid $20,000 so that she would have $5,000 to give away.

The staff at *Ms.* was trying to live their message of equality and respect, both in the office and in the pages of the magazine. This may have been one of the reasons readers had such a strong connection to the publication. For many subscribers, *Ms.* felt like a feminist community, almost as if they were members of a group, rather than just readers. Women shared their thoughts, poetry, fiction, and articles. In the early days, the editors received about five hundred unsolicited manuscripts each week, as well as another four hundred suggestions for the No Comment column, which featured sexist and offensive advertisements sent in by readers. The editors published as many different voices as they could; more than five hundred writers contributed to the magazine in its first years.

Steinem enjoyed reading the letters from subscribers. "I remembered many, many women who said they felt 'crazy' or 'alone' until they found *Ms.* on their newsstands," Steinem said. Some readers said they had asked their husbands to read *Ms.* and felt it helped their marriages. Others said the magazine gave them the courage to leave.

Readers also weighed in with their complaints and suggestions. Some readers complained that the magazine was too radical; others objected because it was too conservative. Some accused it of being too elitist; others found it was too middle-class. Some considered the tone too anti-male; others protested that it was not pro-female enough. Some thought there were too many articles about lesbianism; others wished for more coverage of homosexuality. Despite the criticism, a growing number of readers must have liked what they were seeing: In the first few years, the number of subscribers rose to two hundred thousand per year, plus another two hundred thousand in newsstand sales.

Of course, there were plenty of skeptics and critics. Television reporter Harry Reasoner said, "I'll give it six months before they run out of things to say." Columnist James J. Kilpatrick wrote that *Ms.* magazine was like "C-sharp on an untuned piano . . . a note of petulance, of bitchiness, or nervous fingernails screeching across a blackboard." Conservative Phyllis Schlafly described *Ms.* as "anti-family, anti-children, and pro-abortion. It is a series of sharp-tongued, high-pitched, whining complaints by unmarried women. They view the home as a prison, and the wife and mother as a slave. . . . Women's lib is a total assault on the role of the American woman as wife and mother, and on the family as the basic unit of society."

At first Steinem found the criticism painful to hear, then she realized that the intensity of the criticism proved the power of the message: *Ms.* magazine was changing the conversation about women's issues. It was an important voice that demanded to be heard.

• • • • • • • •

IN THE EARLY 1970S, when *Ms.* first hit the newsstands, America was experiencing a golden period of feminism, a span of a few years when the women's rights movement thrived and a fair and non-sexist future seemed possible. Congress passed the Equal Rights Amendment in 1972 (although it was never ratified by the states). The Supreme Court's *Roe v. Wade* decision legalized abortion in 1973. About 150 colleges and universities opened women's studies programs and departments by 1975. For the first time, women were talking about equal pay for equal work, sexual harassment, rape, date rape, pornography, domestic violence, incest, abortion, and reproductive rights. Women were no longer accepting discrimination as a matter of course; they were talking about a way to do something to address these problems.

Not surprisingly, these feminist successes were met with backlash. Almost immediately after the Supreme Court legalized abortion in 1973, the Catholic Church founded the National Right to Life Committee to coordinate antiabortion activities. As soon as the ERA moved to the states for ratification, conservative Phyllis Schlafly founded her Stop ERA campaign to prevent the amendment from becoming law.

The push and pull of social change was under way. Steinem appreciated the need for *Ms.* magazine to represent the feminist point of view, but she didn't necessarily want to be the person to run it. "I wanted there to be a feminist magazine, but I didn't want to do it," Steinem said. She remembered telling a friend, "I'll do this for two years, no longer."

Patricia Carbine and Gloria Steinem pose with a mockup of the
cover of the fifth anniversary issue of *Ms.* magazine

CHAPTER 22

ADVERTISING

Over the years, I spent more time persuading advertisers than editing or writing.

— GLORIA STEINEM

Ms. magazine had no trouble finding readers or writers or story ideas, but it always struggled to find advertisers. Most advertisers weren't eager to support a feminist magazine, and without steady ad revenue, it was hard to make ends meet financially.

From the beginning, Gloria Steinem and Patricia Carbine knew it was going to be difficult to find advertisers. They also knew that without ad income, they would have to charge high subscription rates, and some readers would not be able to afford the magazine. They also believed that part of their mission was to reform the advertising industry by featuring ads that treated women with respect. Instead of forgoing advertising, they created an advertising policy that called for ads that "respect[ed] women's judgment and intelligence."

"When *Ms.* began, we didn't consider not taking ads," Steinem said. "The most important reason was to keep the price of a feminist magazine low enough for most women to afford. But the second and almost equal reason was to provide a forum where women and advertisers could talk to each other and experiment with non-stereotyped, informative, imaginative ads."

They wanted to lead by example and show the world what kind of messages appealed to strong, independent female consumers. That would have been challenging enough, but the magazine adopted policies that made it even more difficult to sell ads for *Ms.* than for other women's magazines.

Ms. priced their ad space drastically higher than that of other women's publications. The cost of advertising is based on the number of readers; in 1972, advertisers paid about two dollars per thousand female readers. *Ms.* charged more than five times that amount—about eleven dollars per thousand readers—the same price charged for space in magazines that targeted men. Steinem and Carbine wanted to make the point that women were worth just as much as men—both in the workforce and as consumers—so they decided to charge advertisers the higher "male" rate. They argued that the demographic profile of their readers—age, education, income, and so forth—was closer to *Psychology Today* than *Ladies' Home Journal*, so the ad rates ought to reflect that. Advertising companies didn't buy the argument.

They also approached advertisers that did not usually target females. Instead of the traditional women's advertisers—companies that sold cosmetics, food, and household products—they solicited ads from industries that typically focused on men, such as automobiles, electronics, credit cards, financial services, and liquor.

Steinem thought that *Ms.* might be able to change advertising policies at other publications, too. Their goal was laudable, if impractical. "If *Ms.* could prove that women were important purchasers of 'people products,' just as men were, those advertisers would support other women's magazines, too," Steinem said. She hoped that this would free up women's magazines to treat women as diverse consumers.

Ms. made the process of selling ads even more challenging by imposing strict standards on content. Ads could not be considered demeaning to women. "Carmakers were still draping blondes in evening gowns over the hoods like ornaments that could be bought with the car," Steinem said. "Even in ads for products that only women used, the authority figures were almost always male."

Advertisers in most women's magazines demanded "complementary copy," which meant editorial content that reinforced the ads. For example, food manufacturers expected recipes using their products next to their ads, and cosmetic companies wanted articles on makeup tips near their ads for eye shadow or blush. *Ms.* refused to publish complementary copy, but it still wanted to include ads for food, cosmetics, and household products. "Publishing ads only for gender-neutral products would give the impression that women have to become 'like men' in order to succeed," Steinem said. After all, feminists eat food, wear makeup, and clean their houses, too.

Instead of complementary copy, *Ms.* published articles about subject matter that some advertisers said created a "hostile editorial environment." For example, *Ms.* covered tough topics, such as rape, incest, abortion, genital mutilation, and domestic violence. No advertiser wanted its product associated with these difficult stories, no matter how important they were to readers.

In other words, advertisers were asked to pay five times more to buy space in an unproven publication with challenging subject matter and without complementary text and then adapt the ads from an existing campaign just for the privilege of advertising in *Ms.*

One more obstacle: The magazine had an all-female sales staff at a time when most ad representatives were male. These women regularly faced rejection and often encountered outright hostility on their sales calls. One ad saleswoman went to an appointment at an ad agency, only to have the man who booked the appointment say, "I wouldn't buy a page in your lesbian rag if you paid me. I just wanted to see what a lesbian looked like."

She was stunned. Then he said, "You don't look like a lesbian."

That same ad representative remembered selling an ad for Bulova watches, only to see the ad and realize that it couldn't be published. The ad campaign—designed to appeal to women—showed two kids left waiting in front of a school, waiting for their mother to pick them up. The tagline read, "If Mommy had worn a Bulova . . ."

Steinem knew that advertising was going to be a problem, but she hadn't anticipated that skyrocketing operating costs would make it even harder to balance the budget. In the magazine's first year, the price of paper rose 20 percent, the cost of ink increased 40 percent, and postage jumped by 60 percent. These were factors that could not be controlled.

The editorial staff wasn't paid much. Steinem and Carbine often returned their salaries, but that didn't help balance the budget. The magazine earned a profit for the first time in 1974, and it lost money most of the time after that.

. . . .

STEINEM BECAME THE embodiment of *Ms.* Many advertisers and prospective investors insisted on meeting with Steinem, often out of curiosity rather than real interest in buying an ad or investing money. Steinem used her fame to generate publicity for the magazine. She continued to speak around the country, always doing publicity for the magazine at the same time.

The work was exhausting. Steinem was trapped in what seemed like an endless, mostly thankless, cycle of soliciting advertisers and raising money for *Ms.*, rather than writing and creating projects of her own. "Over the years, I spent more time persuading advertisers than editing or writing," Steinem said.

The magazine barely scraped by most months, so Steinem never felt she had time to rest or celebrate her accomplishments.

As soon as the bills were paid one month, she had to start hustling for the next deadline. By that point she realized that she had become a one-issue writer—her writing was now associated solely with the women's movement—but this didn't bother her as much as she had feared because she still had so much to say.

The 1970s held many triumphs and
challenges for Gloria Steinem
[Everett Collection/Alamy]

CHAPTER 23

CIA
BACKLASH

I took no orders at all from the US government in any of its forms or agencies.

— GLORIA STEINEM

While distracted with keeping *Ms.* magazine holding on month to month, Gloria Steinem was blindsided—as well as hurt—in 1975 when a group of feminists she thought were her allies called a press conference to accuse her of working for the Central Intelligence Agency (CIA) to undermine the women's movement. The group issued a sixteen-page press release titled "Redstockings Disclose Gloria Steinem's CIA Cover-up."

Steinem was stunned. The story was old news: Eight years before, in 1967, the leftist political magazine *Ramparts* had reported that the CIA had channeled money to several student organizations, including the Independent Research Service, where Steinem had worked after returning from India. When the article came out, her former boss at the IRS, George Abrams, called Steinem to ask if she was willing to talk to reporters. "I'm fine," Steinem said. "I'll take the heat on this."

Without apology, Steinem appeared on Walter Cronkite's evening news program and explained that the youth festivals were international gatherings used to spread Soviet propaganda. Her employer—the Independent Research Service—helped American students attend the festivals, not to promote Communism but to showcase democracy.

In another interview, Steinem told the *New York Times* that it was common for other governments to fund student delegates at these events. She explained that in the late 1950s and early 1960s the country was still recovering from the anti-Communist fear stirred up by the McCarthy hearings, so no private industry or branch of government would openly fund anything remotely associated with a communist youth festival. "Far from being shocked by this involvement, I was happy to find some liberals in government in those days who were farsighted and cared enough to get Americans of all political views to the festival," Steinem told the *New York Times*. She added that the "CIA's big mistake was not supplanting itself with private funds fast enough."

Steinem said she didn't know about the CIA connection to the Independent Research Service at the time she took the job. She insisted that the CIA never told the students what to say or asked them to spy or report on any other Americans or foreign nationals. The CIA "wanted to do what we wanted to do—present a healthy, diverse view of the United States," Steinem told a reporter from the *Washington Post*.

What seemed innocent in 1959 seemed questionable by 1967 because in the intervening years the public had grown suspicious of the CIA. People distrusted the CIA because they had learned about ways the group had acted against citizens and governments around the world. From Steinem's point of view, public perceptions of the CIA weren't relevant: She and her student group hadn't done anything wrong or unpatriotic.

When the story surfaced in 1967, Steinem explained her position to the press, and it went away. When the story resurfaced in 1975, Steinem was surprised that anyone still considered it news. Nothing had changed. She was also shocked that the story was being promoted by the Redstockings, a group of radical feminists, many of whom she considered friends.

The Redstockings press release was hostile to both Steinem and *Ms.* magazine. "Gloria Steinem has a ten-year association with the CIA stretching from 1959 to 1969, which she has misrepresented and covered up," the press release charged. "Furthermore, we have become convinced that *Ms.* magazine, founded and edited by her, is hurting the women's liberation movement."

The Redstockings accused Steinem of being the CIA's secret weapon to sabotage the women's movement. They argued that

Steinem's less radical form of feminism distracted from the authentic voice of their group and that the CIA sometimes created parallel organizations to provide an alternative to radicalism. Steinem's "watered down" voice—a form of Feminism Lite—was the CIA's inoculation against full-force feminist radicalism. Although they did not offer any proof or evidence to back their claim, the Redstockings also alleged that *Ms.* magazine and the Women's Action Alliance collected names and information about people in the movement and shared it with the CIA.

The timing of the press conference was suspect. Steinem's connection to the CIA was discussed in a chapter of *Feminist Revolution*, a book the Redstockings were about to release. The Redstockings said they were announcing the Steinem material early "because of its pressing importance," but Steinem and others thought it was a way to try to get publicity for their book release by exploiting the famous feminist's name.

In addition to publicizing the book, some people have questioned if the press release was also intended to be a personal attack against Steinem. Redstockings leader Kathie Sarachild had actually written a manuscript about consciousness raising that was rejected by the editors at the Ms. Foundation. Steinem said that the editors had found the manuscript unpublishable. Sarachild was told she could keep the advance for the book, unless she published the manuscript elsewhere, but no other publisher was interested in the book. Sarachild blamed Steinem and *Ms.* for her literary failure.

Most mainstream journalists who saw the press release looked into the story and dismissed it. There was nothing new and no compelling evidence that Steinem was ever in cahoots with the CIA.

· · · · · · · ·

WHEN THEY FIRST heard about the press release, Steinem's friends and colleagues thought the claims were absurd. They joked with Steinem and posted a sign on the door to the *Ms.* office that read WELCOME TO THE CIA.

But Steinem took the criticism seriously. She didn't want to do anything that could compromise *Ms.* or bring negative attention to the magazine. She also let the harsh words get under her skin because she had respected the Redstockings, and she wanted their respect in return. Steinem expected to be attacked from the right, but she wasn't prepared to be accused of wrongdoing by the people she had thought were her colleagues. These fellow feminists were attacking Steinem's core identity, her fundamental sense of self.

Steinem's coworkers were shocked at how seriously she took the accusations. She asked her closest friends what they thought she should do. Most said to ignore the issue and wait for it to pass.

But Steinem couldn't let it go. She kept silent from May to July 1975, and then she decided to respond, but only in the feminist press. She wrote a six-page, single-spaced letter and shared it with six feminist newspapers, hoping to keep the discussion limited to feminist circles.

She didn't do herself any favors with her response. There was no debate that Steinem had, in fact, helped run a group backed by the CIA. She had admitted as much in 1967. But there was no indication that she had done anything dishonest or dishonorable. She wasn't a spy. She didn't need to defend herself from unreasonable and false accusations. But once she answered her critics, she gave them more ammunition to use against her.

"I took no orders at all from the US government in any of its forms or agencies," Steinem wrote in her response. "For better or worse, I have always been my own person. I naively believed that the ultimate money source didn't matter, since no control or orders came with it. It's painfully clear with hindsight that even indirect, control-free funding was a mistake, but I didn't realize it then."

Steinem strongly objected to the fact that the Redstockings press release accused her of lying about her childhood and exaggerating her poverty and misfortune, citing comments from her mother, who sometimes denied that she was divorced or that the family had been poor during their time in Toledo. Steinem had asked reporters to leave her mother alone; she was angry that the Redstockings had brought her personal life into their press campaign.

Just as Steinem had feared, her letter was noticed by a *New York Times* reporter, who wrote a three-quarter-page article titled "Dissension Among Feminists: The Rift Widens." The *Washington Post* followed with a long story describing the Redstockings' charges and other attacks on Gloria.

Steinem was heartbroken that the story was blowing up. Her greatest worry was the impact of the controversy on advertisers. What would it mean for *Ms.?*

• • • • • • • •

IT WASN'T JUST Steinem who faced attack from those who disagreed with her. The problem of feminists picking on one another had become significant enough within the women's movement for it to have earned a name: trashing.

In the April 1976 issue of *Ms.*, Jo "Joreen" Freeman republished an earlier essay about the problem. In her article "Trashing," Freeman wrote that she had "been watching for years with increasing dismay as the Movement consciously destroys anyone within it who stands out in any way."

The focus is on the personal, rather than the ideological. "Trashing is a particularly vicious form of character assassination which amounts to psychological rape," Freeman wrote. "It is manipulative, dishonest, and excessive. It is occasionally disguised by the rhetoric of honest conflict, or covered up by denying that any disapproval exists at all. But it is not done to expose disagreement or to resolve differences. It is done to disparage and destroy."

Ms. magazine attempted to address the issue by bringing it out into the light and exploring it. Only through open discussion and debate could the movement and the women in it begin to mend their ways and reunite to work together toward their common good. Steinem hated conflict, but one thing she hated more was women attacking one another. She wanted the women's movement to act in unison when possible, and when that wasn't possible, for women to treat one another with respect and dignity. The women's movement did not always act in unity, but when it did, the results were memorable, as they were in Houston in 1977.

International Women's Day 1975. Gloria Steinem with
Paulene Haines, a representative of the American Indian
Movement, member of the Cherokee Nation

[Keystone Press/Alamy]

CHAPTER 24

HOUSTON

It was the most racially, economically, and generally representative national meeting this country has ever seen.

— GLORIA STEINEM

The women's rights movement wasn't an American phenomenon. During the 1970s, a feminist consciousness spread around the world as people began to recognize and consider the needs and concerns of women in countries all over the globe. The United Nations declared 1975 to be International Women's Year, an act that helped raise questions about the status of women worldwide. "The contagion of feminism is crossing boundaries of space and language," Gloria Steinem said. "Women on every continent are beginning to question their status." Sisterhood was not only powerful but international as well.

In the United States, President Gerald Ford appointed a commission to gather statistics about American women for the international United Nations meeting and to make recommendations about what should be done to improve their lives. This wasn't easy to do because the women's movement didn't have a clearly defined agenda. The central question was deceptively simple: What did women want?

To answer that question, New York congresswoman Bella Abzug drafted legislation to fund a nationwide women's conference that would help American women establish specific goals for the women's movement. "It was a constitutional convention for the female half of the country," Steinem said. "After all, we had been excluded from the first one."

It was a vast undertaking. The legislation that was passed required that every state and territory elect delegates and suggest topics for discussion at a national conference to be held in Houston. At the national event, the delegates would vote on a National Plan of Action, which would become a guide to leaders in Washington, DC, and the states. In other words, the national conference would provide a clear and democratic answer to the question of what women want.

Never before in the nation's history had so many women from so many different states and constituencies gathered with a common goal. "It was . . . the most racially, economically, and generally representative national meeting this country has ever seen," Steinem said. "For example, the Native American women there said they themselves had not come together from so many tribes and nations before."

On March 28, 1977, President Jimmy Carter appointed Abzug as presiding officer of the National Commission on the Observance of International Women's Year. Gloria Steinem was named to the commission, along with several dozen other well-known female leaders, including Maya Angelou, Betty Ford, and Coretta Scott King. For the first time in United States history, federal money would be used to hold a conference for American women.

"I was as scared as I had ever been," Steinem said. "This organizing challenge was a little like a presidential campaign, with a fraction of the resources. It meant helping to create a representative planning body in each state and territory, including groups that had never been together before."

Women were eager to participate. In Alaska, seven thousand women crowded into an auditorium designed for six hundred. In New York, eleven thousand women, four times more than expected, lined up around government buildings in the state capital. The level of interest exceeded all expectations. Women wanted to be heard.

In a number of states, groups opposed to a feminist agenda tried to change the conversation by controlling the election of delegates. For example, only 2 percent of the population in Washington state belonged to the Church of Jesus Christ of Latter-day Saints (the Mormon Church), but the group bused in so many women that half of those attending the state conference were

Mormons. These women were able to elect an unjustified number of delegates to the national convention to represent their point of view. The same disproportionate representation occurred in Michigan and Missouri.

"These state conferences were part of my education about the power and politics of the Mormon Church," Steinem said. "Buses of women would arrive with a man at the head of each who then seated them together and told them how to vote by holding up his hand with a glove on it." These delegates did not vote their conscience; they voted as the male organizer told them to.

Other religious groups also got involved. In Missouri, church buses brought five hundred Christian fundamentalist women and men to the state conference. In many states, Catholic groups came. "I began to see that for some, religion was just a form of politics you couldn't criticize," Steinem said.

Conservative Phyllis Schlafly spoke out against the state and national conferences. "The Commission on International Women's Year is a costly mistake at the taxpayer's expense," Schlafly said. "The whole thing was designed as a media event, a charade to go through the motions of those phony state conferences and national conference in order to pass resolutions that were prewritten and prepackaged . . . to tell the Congress and the States Legislatures that this is what American women want." Schlafly attempted to have her own representatives elected to the delegations so that they could vote against the feminist agenda.

In addition to the federal funding, the conservatives opposed the conferences because they knew that the results of the conference would legitimize the feminist agenda. The women's movement was growing up: It was no longer small groups of women in consciousness-raising groups talking about how they were being treated; it was becoming a national political force that would have the authority and power to influence Congress and state legislators.

The anti-feminist groups organized a significant voting bloc. By the time of the national conference, right-wing groups—religious fundamentalists, right-to-life groups, the Eagle Forum, the John Birch Society, the Ku Klux Klan, among others—had won about 15 to 20 percent of the delegates to the national conference. Their voices would be heard, too.

· · · · · · · ·

THE NATIONAL WOMEN'S CONFERENCE opened on November 18, 1977, when a lighted torch arrived in Houston after having been carried twenty-six hundred miles by women's relay teams from Seneca Falls, New York, the site of the nation's first women's rights convention in 1848. After a series of welcomes and speeches, the two thousand official delegates got to work.

"With issue areas from the arts to welfare, and three days to vote on them, there was a feeling of urgency, excitement, and even a little fear that we couldn't pull it off," Steinem said. The delegates debated and eventually passed twenty-six different multi-issue planks or political positions, including those involving childcare, lesbian rights, economic rights, foreign policy, and health security, among other topics. The topics under consideration had been selected at the state conferences.

About eighteen thousand observers also attended the conference to witness history being made. In addition, hundreds of anti-ERA and antiabortion picketers marched outside the arena. Conservative Schlafly held her own anti-feminist event on the other side of Houston. "Across town, a right-wing and religious counter-conference—led by Phyllis Schlafly—was getting equal media coverage for accusing the National Women's Conference of being antifamily, anti-God, and otherwise unrepresentative," Steinem said. "Never mind that those counter-conference participants had been elected by no one."

Through the hectic activity, some important connections were being made. "In the midst of this chaos, about twenty women delegates from Indian Country were taking matters into their own hands," Steinem said. The Native American women had found one another by putting a hand-lettered notice in the lobby. They gathered in a talking circle in the ladies' lounge because all the meeting rooms were occupied. "Rarely had these women from different and distant parts of Indian Country been able to meet together," Steinem said. "When they told me this, I had my first flash of organizer's pride: *If only this happens, it will be enough.*"

At the conference, Steinem was asked to help draft a resolution from the various women-of-color caucuses. There were women who identified as African American, Latinas, Chinese Americans, Japanese Americans, Filipinas, American Indians, and Pacific Americans from Hawaii, Guam, and Samoa. Steinem acted as a scribe, going from one hotel meeting room to another, taking notes, suggesting language for their approval, and working out compromises. The goal was to write a substitute for the so-called minority women's plank.

Steinem helped define key issues and share draft language

among the various groups. "This was an honor, but it also upped my already high anxiety level," Steinem said. "I was afraid I would mess up. I wasn't even sure I could physically get to each meeting in the midst of conference chaos."

While the groups had unique issues and concerns, they also shared a lot of common goals. The official report on the conference said: "For the first time, minority women . . . were present in such a critical mass that they were able to define their own needs as well as to declare their stake in each women's issue."

Each group had unique concerns. The African American women raised umbrella issues of racism and poverty. The Asian and Pacific American Caucus described challenges of language barriers, sweatshops, and the isolation of women who came to this country as servicemen's wives. The Hispanic Caucus addressed concerns about mothers being deported away from their American-born children. Puerto Ricans complained that they were treated as if they were not American citizens. Cubans worried about being cut off from their families by tensions with their home country. "Somehow, this all had to go into one substitute minority plank that could come to the floor and be voted on by all delegates," Steinem said.

Of all the struggles described by the women, Steinem was most shocked at the issues raised by the American Indian and Alaskan Native Caucus. They spoke about tribal sovereignty and termination of treaties. "I began to realize there were major cultures in my own country of which I knew nothing," Steinem said.

In front of the entire conference, representatives from each of the minority groups took a moment at the microphone to address the delegates and explain the unique concerns facing their populations. The final speaker was Coretta Scott King, who noted that the unemployment rate for young Black women was even higher than that of young Black men; she also discussed the challenges in housing and childcare facing Black families. When she finished with her remarks, King raised her voice above that of the cheering crowd. She said: "Let this message go forth from Houston and spread all over this land. There is a new force, a new understanding, a new sisterhood against all injustice that has been born here. We will not be divided and defeated again!"

The delegates voted to accept the minority plank by acclamation.

"It was the high point of the conference," Steinem said. "I was as proud of my facilitating role as anything I had ever done in my life."

After the vote, someone in the crowd began to sing the civil rights anthem "We Shall Overcome." One by one, the message spread through the arena as people stood, joined hands, and became one voice in song. "I saw a white man and woman from the Mississippi delegation, the group that had been elected as a state conference partly taken over by the [Ku Klux] Klan, reach across neighbors to hold hands and stand," Steinem said. "By the second chorus, the observers in the bleachers and media were standing and singing, too." When the song ended, people raised their clasped hands above their heads and chanted, "It's our movement now!" "No one seemed to want this moment to end," Steinem said.

It was an emotional high point for Steinem. "I was surprised to find myself in tears," she said. "Because these women had trusted me to help as a writer, I began to see a way of bringing together two things—writing and activism—that until then had torn me apart in everyday life."

After the closing ceremony, the crowds thinned and Steinem stood among the empty chairs and wondered what impact, if any, the event would have on the future of the women's movement. She turned and saw three young Native American women walking toward her. One of them carried a red-fringed shawl with a border of purple and gold, and a second held a beaded necklace with a large blue-and-white flower medallion. They wrapped the shawl over Steinem's shoulders and slipped the necklace over her head, explaining that these items would keep her safe.

Steinem felt honored and humbled by the gesture. "I wore the necklace whenever I had to do something I was afraid of," Steinem said. She found strength when she put it on and eventually wore it out. "I had to preserve the remaining beads in a bowl."

At the end of the three-day event, Steinem felt exhausted but inspired. The women at the conference had worked together and agreed on most of their goals. She had worried that the meeting would fall apart and dissolve into chaos while the world was watching, but that didn't happen. Instead, the effort had helped legitimize and democratize the women's movement. The Houston conference and the fifty-six smaller conferences that led up to it shaped a national agenda and a plan for the women's movement.

For Steinem, the 1977 National Women's Conference was proof that women can achieve great things when they work together. "It may take the prize as the most important event nobody knows about," she said. "My life was changed by a new sense of connection—with issues, possibilities, and women I came to know in the trenches. The conference also brought a huge and diverse movement together around shared issues and values. You might say it was the ultimate talking circle."

Gloria Steinem, photographed in her home, 1977
[Lynn Gilbert/Wikimedia Commons]

CHAPTER 25

OUTSPOKEN

Glory be to God for Gloria!

—Father Harvey Egan

Several months after she returned from the National Women's Conference in Houston, Gloria Steinem received an invitation from Father Harvey Egan to speak at St. Joan of Arc Catholic Church in Minneapolis, Minnesota. Father Egan was known as a maverick priest, a quality Steinem admired. "He himself prays to God the mother to make up for centuries of Catholic priests and popes who pray only to God the father," Steinem said.

As part of his ministry, Father Egan had a tradition of inviting provocative speakers to present homilies to his congregation. Steinem wasn't the first activist or the first woman to accept his offer to speak. Father Egan's goal was to challenge his church to hear different experiences and points of view.

Steinem was skeptical at first. "I'm worried about getting him into even more trouble," she said. But she assumed that Father Egan knew what he was doing. She accepted the invitation, unaware of what kind of trouble she *was* about to cause.

The church leadership had been concerned about Father Egan's choice of speakers, but they accepted his untraditional approach because he was so popular with the liberal Catholics of Minnesota. When he invited her, Father Egan had never met Steinem, although he had heard her speak several years before at the University of Minnesota.

As soon as word got out that Steinem was going to address the congregation, those who objected to her feminist message began to organize. On the day she presented her homily, the church was surrounded by mobs of protesters carrying graphic posters and loudspeakers blaring: "Gloria Steinem is a murderer. Gloria Steinem is a baby-killer."

Steinem took the outside protesters in stride; she had faced down her critics many times before. She was more concerned about facing those inside the church who came to hear her. "Father Egan tells me not to worry, the positive response has been overwhelming," Steinem said. The interest had been so great that Father Egan decided to hold two Masses. "The news that I'll have to speak twice makes me more nervous than the presence of protesters," Steinem said.

Even after years of public speaking, Steinem was terrified to address the crowd. She never expected to speak from a pulpit in a Catholic church. When Father Egan finished introducing her, he lifted his arms so his vestments billowed out like a butterfly and said with a mischievous smile, "Glory be to God for Gloria!"

In her remarks, Steinem did not mention abortion directly, but she did say that the right to have—or not to have—children without government interference was as important as the rights of freedom of speech and assembly. She said that God was present in all living things, including women. And she argued that most institutionalized religions have perpetuated a central message of sexism and racism.

"I am not suggesting to you that God from now on should be a woman," Steinem said. "I am suggesting that there are political motivations for the fact that God, in our memories, has been a man—usually a white man—and that the function of the great religions of the world has very often been to support, enshrine, and make sacred this concept and system." In other words, the church is an example of a patriarchal institution designed to control women.

Steinem's speech sparked a nationwide outcry. Archbishop John Roach, Father Egan's superior in the church, called Steinem's speech an affront to the church; he reprimanded Father Egan for inviting her and announced that future lay speakers would require the approval of the church.

Other church leaders spoke out in Father Egan's defense. For example, Rev. George H. Martin of Saint Luke's Parish in Minneapolis wrote to the *Minneapolis Star* (September 23, 1978) defending Steinem's homily and noting, "If we listen only to people who agree with us we shall become as mild as milk toast and as meek as lambs." Father Martin also wrote directly to Steinem to tell her she would be welcome to speak at his Episcopalian church, "which has been actively seeking to affirm the role of the women in the church." In response to the controversy, some people left Father Egan's church, but many more joined.

It turned out that echoes of Steinem's fiery words reached all the way to the Vatican. A few weeks after her address, Steinem opened the *New York Times* and read the front-page headline, "Pope Forbids Homilies by Laypeople." She was stunned. "Nothing in my life quite prepare[d] me for feeling directly addressed by the pope," Steinem said. Steinem wasn't mentioned by name, but it was clear that her remarks prompted the papal response.

Father Egan respected the papal decision, but he didn't want to give up his popular program. He tried to get around the ruling on a technicality by renaming the homily "a Sunday presentation." When Father Egan retired ten years later, St. Joan of Arc was the most popular Catholic church in Minnesota.

Gloria Steinem with Mort Zuckerman. January 22, 1986

[New York Post Archives/Getty Images]

CHAPTER 26

STATUS
CHANGES

Ms. *is the exception among women's magazines.*

—GLORIA STEINEM

In addition to the stress of her conflict with the Catholic Church, by the late 1970s Gloria Steinem had to face the reality that *Ms.* magazine was losing money month after month and something had to be done. At the time, *Ms.* had more than five hundred thousand subscribers, but despite the rising circulation numbers and the valiant efforts of the ad sales staff, the magazine couldn't attract enough advertisers to break even.

Steinem and Patricia Carbine considered their options. They could look for investors and risk losing control of the magazine, or they could sell it. Steinem approached Katharine Graham, publisher of the *Washington Post*, to see if she might consider buying the magazine, but Graham wasn't interested. She did warn Steinem to be careful because most investors would turn *Ms.* into a conventional women's magazine.

Steinem and Carbine considered one other option: The magazine could become a nonprofit publication as a subsidiary of the Ms. Foundation for Women. Becoming a nonprofit had a number of benefits: *Ms.* could remain solidly feminist; it could accept tax-deductible donations; and its mailing costs would decrease considerably because nonprofits had less expensive mailing rates at the time. After reflection, Steinem, Carbine, and investor Warner Communications decided that becoming a nonprofit was the only viable solution.

• • • • • • • •

IN AUGUST 1979, the Internal Revenue Service approved of the status change and *Ms.* magazine became the public information arm of the Ms. Foundation for Women. Steinem, Carbine, and Warner Communications donated their stock to the new nonprofit.

In the pages of *Ms.*, Steinem explained to readers how the nonprofit status would allow the magazine to advocate for social change with a goal of educating readers, not making a profit. "This new status is a recognition of the true educational value in both past efforts and future plans," Steinem wrote. "It confirms once again that *Ms.* is the exception among women's magazines."

As a nonprofit, the magazine could now accept donations. The first foundation grant to *Ms.* came from the owner and publisher of the *New York Post*, who gave $200,000. This qualified *Ms.* for a matching grant from the Ford Foundation. This infusion of money saved the magazine from collapse.

Becoming a nonprofit didn't do anything to lure new advertisers. The magazine continued to struggle month to month, cobbling together just enough money to make ends meet. When postage rates climbed, they had no choice but to raise subscription rates.

In addition to the financial struggles, *Ms.* also faced a new wave of attacks from political opponents. Right-wing groups attempted to get *Ms.* banned from high school libraries. The first place this happened was in Nashua, New Hampshire, in 1978. In that case, the local court overruled the ban. In 1980, Baptist and Mormon groups in Contra Costa, California, outside San Francisco, organized a broad coalition to force the school board to ban *Ms.* from the high school.

"*Ms.* would be rated 'X' if it was a movie," said one of the leaders of the effort. She argued that *Ms.* made students "experts in sex. They know a homosexual from a heterosexual. And they can tell a bisexual from a lesbian!" In that case, the school board reached a compromise: *Ms.* could remain in the library, but high school students would need to get permission from both a parent and a teacher to check it out.

• • • • • • • •

IN HER PERSONAL LIFE, Steinem also went through a status change when she began to date multimillionaire real-estate developer Mortimer Zuckerman. He didn't have Steinem's national public profile, but Zuckerman was well-known in New York and Boston business and social circles. They first met in the late 1970s at a National Women's Political Caucus fund-raiser held in Zuckerman's Boston home. They began seeing each other several years later, and by the mid-1980s the couple had become a staple in gossip columns and New York tabloids.

The relationship dumbfounded many of Steinem's closest friends, who didn't think she and Zuckerman were well suited for each other. Zuckerman was undeniably smart; Steinem told her friends he was the smartest man she had ever met. He had earned law degrees from McGill University in Canada and Harvard University in Boston, as well as a master's in business administration from the Wharton School of Business at University of Pennsylvania. When he started his career, he held an entry-level position at a real-estate firm, but within seven months, he was the chief financial officer. In 1969, he started his own firm and made a fortune. He was fascinated by the media, so he bought several publications, including *U.S. News & World Report* and the *Atlantic Monthly*.

At first, Steinem and Zuckerman also had fun together. They enjoyed dancing and debating and spending weekends in the Hamptons. They both worked hard, and when they took time to relax, they enjoyed time together.

Zuckerman contributed to *Ms.* financially. He guaranteed several loans to the magazine and donated about four hundred thousand dollars, for a total of $1.4 million in support. He offered to have his experts look at the overall operation and provide suggestions, but Steinem turned him down because she didn't want him telling her what to do.

While the accounts of their relationship vary, it's likely that they discussed getting married. According to Steinem, Zuckerman talked about marriage, and she didn't tell him she wasn't interested. They also talked about having a baby. Steinem said the baby issue may have reflected a misunderstanding in a conversation about her fertility. She was fifty years old at the time of their relationship, and she believed if she conceived a child the pregnancy would almost certainly end in miscarriage. "I was at fault for not looking him in the eye and saying that I wouldn't do this [have a baby] even if I were twenty-two," Steinem said. Instead of clarifying her feelings about the issue, she explained that it was almost impossible for her to get pregnant at her age. "He took this to mean I would if I could," she said. Steinem thought having a baby was just a fantasy on his part.

In hindsight, Steinem recognized that the relationship may not have been good for her. She later wrote that she had played down who she was and played up who he wanted her to be to make Zuckerman fall in love with her. He said that he appreciated her intelligence but felt exhausted by her tendency to interpret everything he said or did in ideological terms. Whenever he returned home from a business trip, he wondered what he had done that Steinem was going to say had been morally wrong. He told Steinem that living with a saint was harder than being one.

"Having for the first time in my life made a lover out of a man who wasn't a friend first—my mistake, not his, since I was the one being untrue to myself—I had a huge stake in justifying what I had done," Steinem said.

They dated exclusively for about two and a half years and dated but saw other people for another year and a half. Unlike almost every other relationship in her past, when the affair with Zuckerman ended, it did not become a friendship. "I felt I was walking on eggs all the time . . . By two years after we were seeing each other, I had given up on the idea that if this man became a happier person he would also become a nicer one," Steinem said. "I realized, as so many women have, that the idea that I could 'change' a man was the female version of a fantasy of power."

• • • • • • • •

THE UNITED STATES government also went through a status change of its own in 1980. That year, conservative Republican Ronald Reagan was elected president, running on an anti-feminist, conservative platform. He campaigned on the promise of support for a constitutional amendment banning abortion, the appointment of antichoice judges, and the defeat of the Equal Rights Amendment.

The 1970s were over, and the feminist backlash had begun.

Gloria with her mother, Ruth, circa the 1970s
[Gloria Steinem Papers/Sophia Smith Collection, Smith College]

CHAPTER 27

GOODBYE, RUTH

Dying seems less sad than having lived too little.

— GLORIA STEINEM

Gloria Steinem was the face of feminism for much of the country, so, not surprisingly, she became a target of those who criticized the women's movement. She took the blows, accepting them as part of her role as a public figure, but Steinem tried to keep her private life private, in part to protect her mentally ill mother, Ruth.

Steinem had always tried to look after Ruth. As a young girl, Steinem stayed by her mother's side and comforted her during episodes of fear and confusion. As a young woman, Steinem worked with her sister to make sure that their mother's needs were met and that she felt safe. As an adult, Steinem tried to keep reporters from looking into her mother's life in ways that could cause her distress. As an older woman, Steinem kept watch over her mother, who remained fragile, even though her mental health had stabilized to the point that she could live in an apartment by herself, work at a part-time job, and join an Episcopal church that worked with the poor and homeless.

Unfortunately, reporters did not honor Steinem's requests for privacy. In the 1970s, as Steinem became a voice of the women's movement, her life came under public scrutiny. In interviews Steinem told stories of living with her mother in a rat-infested apartment behind a furnace room. Sometimes reporters questioned Ruth about the past, and she felt humiliated and exposed, which increased her anxiety and vulnerability. She was ashamed of this time in their lives and sometimes denied Steinem's claims. Ruth didn't want to remember their past that way. Being the mother of a feminist superstar proved to be emotionally challenging for Ruth.

· · · · · · · ·

RUTH STEINEM SPENT a lot of time in the care of Susanne, Gloria's older sister. While Steinem was establishing herself as a writer in New York City, Susanne, her husband, Bob, and their six children made a home for Ruth, starting in 1964. It wasn't always easy:

Ruth could be difficult and demanding, often insisting that she be engaged with other people in conversation.

The dynamic in the household shifted in 1975 when Susanne, at age fifty, decided to go to law school. She continued to care for her family, but Susanne claimed more time for herself and her needs. In order to find a quiet place to study, she often sat alone in the family's orange Volkswagen bus parked in front of the house. Her children knew where she was, so she could have some separation but still be available if Ruth or one of her children needed her.

Instead of supporting her daughter's dream to become a lawyer, Ruth rebelled. She told her grandchildren that their mother was neglecting her family by returning to school. She complained that the family was falling apart because they no longer sat down to home-cooked meals. Ruth threatened to call the *New York Times* to "tell them that this was what feminism did: it left old sick women all alone." Despite her mother's complaints, Susanne persevered and became an attorney for the Federal Trade Commission.

As Gloria's fame increased over the years, Ruth took pride in her daughter's achievements. Sometimes Ruth would attend Steinem's speeches and interact with reporters, telling them that she tried to stay out of the way, but "I do occasionally bask in reflected Gloria." Steinem tried to be a good daughter: She visited her mother regularly and vacationed with her every year. She occasionally hired a car and driver so that her mother could explore Washington, DC, without riding buses, which sometimes triggered panic attacks. Steinem did her best to address her mother's needs, without being consumed by them.

• • • • • • • •

WHEN RUTH'S HEALTH began to fail, Steinem and her sister arranged for her to move into a nursing home. In 1980, Ruth had a stroke. A year later, she suffered a heart attack. She died on July 15, 1981, one month before her eighty-third birthday.

Steinem and her sister were at their mother's side when she died. They did not want their mother to die alone, as their father had. Ruth had a long-standing fear that she would slip into a coma that would be mistaken for death; she had asked her daughters to sit with her for a while after she took her last breath to make sure she was really gone before accepting that she was dead. On the day their mother died, the sisters honored their mother's request, sitting vigil in the silent room.

• • • • • • • •

STEINEM TRIED TO make sense of her mother's life and death in the essay "Ruth's Song." Writing the essay was an important way for Steinem to process her feelings about her mother. "I remember sitting at my old rolltop desk a few months after my mother died," Steinem wrote. "Those unsaid words must have been stored up in me. I'm a slow and laborious writer, but for this one and only time in my life, the words, even the structure . . . seemed already to exist." Steinem finished writing the essay, but she couldn't bear to read it for years.

In the essay, Steinem interpreted her mother's life from a feminist point of view. Steinem argued that her mother's mental illness may have been, in part, an inevitable consequence of the limitations society placed on women of her time. Her mother longed to be a writer and a newspaper reporter, but she surrendered her career to meet the expectations of her husband and family. Her mother may have married the wrong man and remained in the relationship for the wrong reasons, only to find divorce a shameful symbol of her failure as a wife and mother.

"I know I will spend the next years figuring out what her life has left in me," Steinem wrote. She respected the sacrifices her mother made to make a better life possible for both of her daughters. "It was she who sold that Toledo house, the only home she had, with the determination that the money be used to start me in college. She gave both her daughters the encouragement to leave home for four years of independence that she herself had never had."

Steinem mourned for the life her mother didn't get a chance to live. "I miss her, but perhaps no more in death than I did in life," Steinem wrote. "Dying seems less sad than having lived too little."

Steinem said that she did not revisit the essay until she began to pull together stories she wanted to include as a chapter in her book *Outrageous Acts and Everyday Rebellions*. She wasn't ready to publicly share some of the essays in the book while her mother was alive, but several years after her mother's death Steinem was ready to share some of her most personal stories with her readers.

Gloria signs her book
Outrageous Acts and Everyday Rebellions, 1983
[Duane Howell/Getty Images]

CHAPTER 28

OUTRAGEOUS

What outrageous act will I do today?

—GLORIA STEINEM

G loria Steinem had wanted to write a book for years. "Any male writer my age I know has written at least one book," she said when she was in her early forties. "I haven't written any. I never took control of a whole year or two of my life and said, 'This is what I want to do.'"

Steinem thought she was going to set aside the time to write a book-length manuscript in 1978, when she was chosen as a fellow at the Woodrow Wilson International Center for Scholars at the Smithsonian Institution in Washington, DC. She won the fellowship based on her proposal to write a study of the impact of feminism on political theory, specifically how feminist theory can come from female experience. She thought the structure of the fellowship program would help her stay in one place and concentrate. But Steinem wasn't one to sit still or to be constrained by the rules.

Instead of spending most of her time in Washington, DC, Steinem often returned to New York to work at *Ms.* She continued to accept public speaking engagements and to attend events in support of various feminist organizations. And she spent time with the people she cared about. She considered the culture of Washington and the Wilson Center to be too conservative and stiff for her to do her best work.

The executives at the Wilson Center became frustrated with Steinem for spending much of her time in New York because she was supposed to be part of a community of fellows; one of the objectives of the program was to generate a collegiate atmosphere with daily lunches and frequent seminars. She found these encounters exasperating; too often the men—almost all white men—turned to her to ask about the "women's point of view" on every issue.

"I have nightmares of sitting there for a year and not producing anything," Steinem said. She worried that such a failure would disgrace all women, as well as nonacademics. "That's probably exactly the kind of pressure I need to get myself back to writing again," Steinem said.

While Steinem did not complete a work on feminist theory during her time at the Wilson Center, she did finish several articles, including "The International Crime of Genital Mutilations," which she cowrote with Robin Morgan, and later turned into a piece in *Ms.* The essay was also included as a chapter in the book Steinem did finish a few years later.

In 1983, Steinem completed *Outrageous Acts and Everyday Rebellions*, a collection of twenty-six of her articles, plus two new pieces. The book celebrated Steinem's feminist view of the world, and it captured her witty, compassionate, and sometimes irreverent voice. Within weeks it became a national bestseller.

The title of the book refers to a challenge she extended to audience members at the end of her various speeches. She called it her organizer's deal. "If each person in the room promises that in the twenty-four hours beginning the very next day she or he will do at least *one outrageous* thing in the cause of simple justice, then I promise I will, too," Steinem said. She explained that the act could be large or small: It could be calling a strike or simply telling a partner, "Pick it up yourself." If everyone acted out in the name of justice, one day later the world wouldn't be quite the same. It would also start a revolution: "We will have such a good time that we will never again get up in the morning saying, '*Will* I do anything outrageous?' but only '*What* outrageous act will I do today?'"

• • • • • • • •

ONE OF STEINEM'S most outrageous acts was sharing some of the more intimate details of her early personal life. "Ruth's Song (Because She Could Not Sing It)," one of the chapters in *Outrageous*

Acts, is a version of the essay Steinem wrote in an emotional out-pouring after her mother's death. It is Steinem's feminist interpre-tation of her mother's life and death. "I still don't understand why so many, many years passed before I saw my mother as a person, and before I understood that many of the forces in her life were patterns women share," Steinem wrote. "Like a lot of daughters, I couldn't afford to admit that what had happened to my mother was not all personal or accidental. It would have meant admitting it could happen to me."

Steinem had often wanted to write about her personal life, but she hadn't done so because she was afraid it could hurt her mother. "While she was alive, I couldn't talk about any but the most rou-tine, sanitized, good-news parts of our life together," Steinem said. "There was also her reluctance to admit that we had ever been poor . . . so a great deal of life was off-limits." Steinem wrote that her mother hated when reporters said that the family had lived in a house trailer. "Couldn't they at least say 'vacation mobile home'?" Ruth asked.

When she was an adult, Steinem asked her mother's doctors for a diagnosis that would define Ruth's condition. "They could not identify any serious mental problem and diagnosed her only as having 'an anxiety neurosis': low self-esteem, a fear of being dependent, a terror of being alone, a constant worry about money," Steinem wrote. "She also had spells of what now would be called agoraphobia, a problem almost entirely confined to dependent women: fear of going outside the house, and incapacitating anxi-ety attacks in unfamiliar or public places."

These answers didn't satisfy Steinem's desire to understand her mother's behavior. "Would you say, I asked one of her doctors, that her spirit had been broken? 'I guess that's as good a diagnosis as any,' he said. 'And it's hard to mend anything that's been broken for twenty years.'"

Steinem ended her essay with resignation rather than resolution. She regretted that her mother never had the chance to live the life she wanted, but she now saw Ruth's life in much broader terms. Ruth was Steinem's mother, but she was also a surrogate for all women who did not have the chance to live their dreams. Her mother's life exemplified the high cost of confining women to the domestic sphere and defining them only as wives and mothers. "At least we're now asking questions about all the Ruths in all our family mysteries," she wrote.

· · · · · · · ·

ANOTHER OF THE essays in *Outrageous Acts* explored Steinem's feelings about her twenty-fifth reunion at Smith College in 1981. In the essay "College Reunion," Steinem noted that the worst crime a woman can commit at a reunion was to be thin. Steinem, who had felt anxious about her weight but remained thin her entire life, openly discussed her feelings about food. "Since I understand this discomfort with thin people very well (I have always struggled with being overweight and there are only a few minutes each day when I'm not thinking about food), I tried hard to explain that my being thin at the moment didn't mean I wasn't a food junkie, any more than being sober doesn't mean one isn't an alcoholic," Steinem wrote.

In addition to feeling judged about her weight, Steinem had to deal with a mix-up that occurred during the pre-graduation campus parade. The procession included all the returning students, grouped by classes, from oldest to youngest, ending with the women who would graduate the following day. Steinem and another classmate had made several signs for the event. They read:

THE SECOND WAVE OF FEMINISM SALUTES THE FIRST.

WE SURVIVED JOE MCCARTHY—
WE CAN SURVIVE REAGAN AND THE MORAL MAJORITY.

'56 REMEMBERS OUR SISTERS WHO DIED OF ILLEGAL
ABORTIONS. DON'T LET IT HAPPEN AGAIN!

WOMEN GET MORE RADICAL WITH AGE.

These signs were more political than the assigned "Focus '56" theme, which was a play on words because many in the class now needed reading glasses. Still, Steinem didn't think the messages would cause a stir because most of the women in her class agreed with the content of the signs. Surveys had showed that a majority of the class had voted against Reagan and 98 percent favored legal abortion.

As soon as a reunion organizer saw the signs, she marched over and asked Steinem who had authorized the signs, explaining that the slogans had been chosen and approved months in advance. As a compromise, someone suggested that Steinem and those who chose to carry her signs march behind the rest of their class so that their signs wouldn't interfere with the Focus '56 theme. They agreed.

Later, the organizers returned to say that Steinem and her

contingent had to march at the end of the entire parade, meaning they could not march with their class. "With alarmingly little spine left, I agreed," Steinem said.

Steinem and her fellow rebels from the class of 1956 stood on the sidelines, waiting for the parade to pass, when members of the class of 1966 welcomed them into the line. One of the marchers explained that they supported the message because a member of their class had died during an illegal abortion. "It was all hushed up—but we knew," she said.

As they marched, those watching cheered when they spotted Steinem's signs. "When we finally passed in front of the president's house, where the new graduates were waiting, there were special cheers and fists raised in salute from a cluster of young Black graduates, and more applause from other seniors and their families," Steinem said. The new graduates offered hope for a more promising future. "By the time we arrived at our destination in the beautiful, sun-dappled quad, all feelings of conflict had gone."

Steinem reflected on the meaning of her Smith College education, concluding: "I think we deserve to be proud that so many 'Smith girls' of the 1950s survived educations that trained us to fit the world, or at least to fear the conflict that comes from trying to make the world fit us."

• • • • • • • •

STEINEM WENT ON a twenty-six-city, nine-week publicity tour for *Outrageous Acts*. In addition to discussing the book, she promoted *Ms.* and other local feminist organizations whenever possible. She hoped that her successful book tour would translate into increased magazine sales.

The tour hit a snag in October 1983, when an article about Steinem appeared in *People* magazine, accompanied by a two-page photograph of Steinem in a bubble bath, posed with one leg seductively lifted out of the water. Feminists cringed: Why would Steinem—who often complained about being judged for her appearance rather than her ideas—agree to this?

When asked about the photo on the book tour, she said, "Sometimes people confuse feminists with nuns." She explained that the problem with female exploitation wasn't about sexuality but consent, and she had willingly agreed to the photograph.

She later explained how the idea for the photograph had evolved. "Well, it maybe was not the smartest thing I ever did, but it just seemed natural because the photographer from *People* magazine was a wonderful woman traveling with me on a speaking tour," Steinem said. The photographer said all of her images were of Steinem sitting and talking or signing books. She asked if she jogged or played tennis. When asked what she does to relax, Steinem said, "I take a hot bath."

The photographer asked if she could take a photo "if I promise that it will be as decent as any other photo."

"I said sure, because it seemed real," Steinem said. She hadn't considered the way it could be misinterpreted, a mistake she rarely made.

• • • • • • • •

ONLY A FEW months after the release of *Outrageous Acts and Everyday Rebellions*, Steinem turned fifty. Ten years before, a reporter learned it was her birthday, and had said, "You don't look forty."

She famously replied, "This is what forty looks like. We've been lying so long, who would know?" She used the same line again at fifty.

Steinem's fiftieth birthday was marked by a grand fund-raiser for the Ms. Foundation. At the party she was celebrated by more than seven hundred well-wishers, who paid $250 each to attend. The guests included political figures, celebrities, and journalists, as well as some corporate sponsors. Bette Midler performed, Phil Donahue served as emcee, and an all-woman band played into the night.

Newsweek covered the event, describing Steinem as "a dashing role model, the adventurous aunt who inspires others to follow her off the high diving board." Steinem wore a lavender gown and a rhinestone-studded serpent bracelet on her upper arm. One of the partygoers reported that she looked "younger, thinner, and blonder than ever."

At one point in the evening, Steinem addressed the crowd, thanking people, especially her sister, Susanne, for "doing so many things for me that our parents simply couldn't do, things big sisters shouldn't have to do, but who never made me feel it was a burden." She reminded everyone to have fun because, "as Emma Goldman said, 'If you can't dance, it's not my revolution.'"

* * * * * * * *

STEINEM DIDN'T SLOW down at fifty. In the summer of 1985, she finished another book, *Marilyn: Norma Jean*, a photobiography of Marilyn Monroe. She had written about Monroe in the 1972 issue of *Ms.*, as well as in an essay in *Outrageous Acts*. Photographer George

Barris had taken photographs of Monroe in 1962, just before she died, and Steinem's publisher asked her to write the text to accompany the images.

More than forty books had been written about Monroe, all by men. Steinem wanted to examine Monroe's life through a feminist lens as well as a camera lens. She also had practical reasons for agreeing to the project: *Ms.* owed money to the publisher for copies of *Outrageous Acts* that the magazine had used as an incentive to subscribers, so Steinem decided to write the manuscript as repayment of the magazine's debt.

"I think women can learn from her because she's an exaggerated version of what can happen to us," Steinem said. "We're valued for who we are on the outside, and not for our heads and hearts."

Writing the book allowed Steinem to explore some of the issues in her own life. Both she and Monroe had mothers with mental illness and fathers who weren't around much. They both became public figures, objects of the fantasies of their fans and judgment of their critics.

When describing Monroe, Steinem seemed to be describing her own feelings of attachment to the families of the men she dated. "The lifestyle and relatives that came with a particular man seemed to attract her more, and to survive longer, than the man himself," Steinem wrote. "One of the consistencies of her life was this habit of attaching herself to other people's families."

Unlike Steinem, Monroe wanted to have a child. She had had several abortions when she was single, but when she was married to Arthur Miller she tried unsuccessfully to have a baby. Monroe was also terrified of aging. "The restriction of her spirit in the airtight prison of her beauty was so complete that she literally feared aging more than death itself," Steinem wrote.

In her final interview with a reporter before her death, Monroe begged to be taken seriously. "We are all brothers," Monroe said, arguing that the world needs to break down its divisions of race, religion, and class. "Please don't make me a joke," Monroe said to the reporter. "End the interview with what I believe."

"We are too late," Steinem wrote. "We cannot know whether we could have helped Norma Jean Baker or the Marilyn Monroe she became. But we are not too late to do as she asked. At least, we can take her seriously."

Steinem invited readers to see Monroe differently. "Now that women's self-vision is changing, we are thinking again about the life of Marilyn Monroe," she wrote. "Might our new confidence in women's existence with or without the approval of men have helped a thirty-six-year-old woman of talent to stand on her own? To stop depending on sexual attractiveness as the only proof that she was alive—and therefore to face aging with confidence?" Steinem wanted to reconsider the meaning of Monroe's life so that we could redefine the meaning of our own.

• • • • • • • •

WHEN *MARILYN: NORMA JEAN* was published in 1986, Steinem was exhausted. She hadn't been taking care of herself, and she lived with the chronic stress of trying to keep *Ms.* magazine solvent. "We'd been living on the edge of bankruptcy for years, trying to keep it going," Steinem said. "I felt responsible for others. For the foundation, other organizations, fund-raising. I don't know how I survived it."

That year she recruited Wilma Pearl Mankiller, the principal chief of the Cherokee Nation, to the board of directors of the Ms. Foundation. From the moment the two women met, Steinem felt a strong connection, as if she were "sheltered by a strong and timeless tree." When she was with Mankiller, Steinem felt more like her truest self. "Just being with her made it hard not to be as authentic and shit-free as she was."

The two women became trusted friends. At one of Mankiller's first board meetings with the Ms. Foundation, the group had too little money to give to meet the needs of the many rape crisis centers asking for help. After the meeting, Mankiller shared a story she hadn't told before: When she was a young girl, Mankiller had been sexually assaulted by a group of teenage boys in a movie theater near her housing project in San Francisco. "Only sitting in a circle of women, listening to similar stories, allowed her to realize that she wasn't alone," Steinem said.

"From then on, I realized she had said yes to joining us [on the Ms. Foundation] for a reason, conscious or not," Steinem said. Mankiller needed the strength of a group of supportive women. Steinem later spent a winter holiday with Mankiller and her husband in Mexico. At the end of the trip, Mankiller said, "This is the first time in my life that I've been with people who didn't need anything from me." Steinem and Mankiller shared that sometimes overwhelming feeling of being consumed by the needs and demands of people who turned to them for help. The two women valued their friendship in part because they both understood the pressure of being leaders and role models.

For Steinem, the constant and unending pressures of her life began to leave her depleted. In 1986, she started to see a psychother-apist. She initially reached out as part of her research for another book idea, but she soon began talking about her need to find balance in her life. Steinem knew she couldn't sustain her health at the pace she was moving. Something needed to change before it was too late.

Gloria Steinem, 1986
[Ron Galella/Getty Images]

CHAPTER 29

CANCER

I've had a good life.

— GLORIA STEINEM

In May 1986, Gloria Steinem appeared on the *Today* show to promote her latest book, *Marilyn: Norma Jean*. After the program, a producer asked her if she would be willing to substitute as co-anchor for a week in September during host Jane Pauley's maternity leave. Intrigued, Steinem agreed.

Steinem was nervous about appearing on live television, but

she made it through the entire week. When it was over, one of the producers told her she was "Not bad."

She smiled and accepted the compliment. What the producer didn't know—and Steinem still hadn't come to grips with herself—was that the week before, she had been diagnosed with breast cancer.

The Friday before Steinem was to begin her week as coanchor, she went to the doctor for her annual checkup with Dr. Penny Budoff at the Women's Medical Center in Long Island. The previous November, Steinem had visited Dr. Budoff when she had felt a tiny lump in one breast. Steinem had a mammogram, but nothing looked suspicious at the time. Later, the doctor followed up with a sonogram, which also looked clear. At Steinem's September appointment, the surgeon in the practice happened to be in the office instead of at the hospital, so Dr. Budoff suggested that they check the lump with a biopsy, a test that allowed them to remove a sample of tissue and examine it under a microscope.

The lump was so small that the surgeon removed the entire tumor during the biopsy. She "gave me a little Novocain shot, and I sat there and watched her take it out," Steinem said. "It was nothing. I'm grateful I watched, because it makes it much more comprehensible. Otherwise you imagine that it's some sort of terrible thing and there's really this little innocent piece of flesh."

The tissue was sent to the laboratory across the street for a quick look, and the doctors learned that the piece of flesh wasn't at all innocent. The tumor was malignant; Steinem had breast cancer.

"If there is one thing I have taken away from this experience, it is never to trust tests," Steinem said.

On the ride back to her apartment, Steinem remembered thinking: "How interesting. So this is how it's going to end." She reflected on her death, approaching the topic with curiosity. She considered her death as mysterious, not tragic. Her next thought was "I've had a good life."

Rather than feeling fear or regret, Steinem said she felt things were going to be okay. "Such acceptance may sound odd, but I felt those words in every last cell of my being," Steinem said. "It was a moment I won't forget."

Steinem didn't want to die, but she felt it would be okay if that's what happened. "It was all right," she said. "And I valued that. I was really, really grateful for that. Now some of that, I suspect, was that I was so exhausted and worn out and down at the same time. I had come to the end of my ability to continue living the same life anyway."

She told only a few close friends about her diagnosis and asked them not to share the news. She didn't want word to leak out to the press because she was afraid that news of her illness could make it even more difficult for *Ms.* magazine to attract investors and advertisers.

Initially, Steinem chose to be treated at the Memorial Sloan Kettering Cancer Center in New York, but she changed her mind when she overheard her doctor arguing with the surgeon while she was waiting in the exam room. One expert wanted to take out a fourth of her breast to make sure they removed all the cancer, and the other thought the size of the tumor required a less invasive procedure. At the time, the medical community had not reached consensus on the use of a lumpectomy, a less radical surgery in which only the cancerous tissue is removed, rather than the entire breast, underlying muscle, and surrounding lymph nodes.

Steinem had lost confidence in her New York doctors, so she decided to go to Beth Israel Hospital in Boston where she thought the doctors had more experience with lumpectomies. During surgery the doctors found that the margins or edges of Steinem's tumor area were clean, meaning there was little chance that any cancer cells were left behind. A test of the nearby lymph nodes indicated that the cancer had not spread.

A few days after the procedure, Steinem returned to New York to begin six weeks of radiation treatment. To protect her privacy, she registered at the hospital using her grandmother's name, Marie Ochs, the same name she had used when posing as a Playboy Bunny. "Since the [lymph-node] sampling was negative, the rest of the treatment consisted of six weeks of lying like the Bride of Frankenstein on a metal slab each morning while I got radiation treatments," Steinem said. "My self-treatment was much more drastic: doing away with all animal fat in my diet and getting less stress and more sleep."

After completing radiation treatment, Steinem resumed her book tour for *Marilyn: Norma Jean*. She maintained an exhausting schedule, with all-day print, radio, and television interviews and book signings, followed by fund-raisers and events to promote *Ms.* magazine and the Ms. Foundation.

When the treatment was complete, Steinem put thoughts of cancer behind her, although she did try to take better care of herself.

"I was frightened enough by this timely warning to start doing what I needed to do, indeed what I should have been doing all along." Steinem began listening to her body and focusing on her health. "One of the rewards of aging is a less forgiving body that transmits its warnings faster—not as betrayal, but as wisdom," she said. "Cancer makes one listen more carefully, too."

. . . .

STEINEM WALKED WITH other close friends as they faced cancer. "It was Gloria who went with me to all of the doctors and made sure that I did the right thing," said Bella Abzug, who also faced a diagnosis of breast cancer. "No hour was too late. No date was too important. She was there as a human being. As she has been for many."

Wilma Mankiller was also supported by Steinem during several medical challenges. About a year after Mankiller joined the Ms. Foundation board, Steinem worried that her new friend didn't look well. In a private moment, Steinem asked, "What's wrong with you, and what can I do?"

Mankiller said that her kidneys were failing. Her doctor wanted to remove both kidneys and put her on dialysis while waiting for a transplant. Steinem offered to help connect her with a kidney expert. Mankiller didn't want to consult another doctor, but Steinem persisted, following up with her again and again. Mankiller eventually agreed to see the doctor Steinem recommended, and, she credited him—and Steinem's perseverance—with saving her life. "She just kept bothering me until I called the doctor," Mankiller said.

As she continued to support her friends, Steinem put her own health concerns behind her and moved forward with her work. In the fall of 1986, Steinem focused her attention on another pressing problem: Once again *Ms.* magazine was losing money at an unsustainable rate. Something had to be done.

Gloria Steinem and Patricia Carbine,
cofounders of *Ms.* magazine. May 7, 1987.
[Angel Franco/New York Times Co./Getty Images]

CHAPTER 30

SELLING AND BUYING *MS.*

Ms. has found a new way of publishing by proving that readers will pay for what they really want.

—GLORIA STEINEM

By the spring of 1987, Gloria Steinem and Patricia Carbine decided that they had run out of options. They realized that the only way to save *Ms.* magazine was to sell it. That summer they found who they thought were the ideal buyers: two feminists—Sandra Yates and Anne Summers—who worked for a well-financed Australian media company.

The decision to sell came with both relief and regret. "It's very sad—but also better than being bought for our subscription list and folded into a traditional magazine," said Steinem. "These are two good women who want to do their best to keep *Ms.*'s feminist spirit."

In November 1987, Fairfax Publications (US) Ltd. bought *Ms.* from the Ms. Foundation for Education and Communication for about ten million dollars, part cash and part the assumption of the magazine's debts. After the bills were paid, the Ms. Foundation cleared about three million dollars. Steinem and Carbine, who had donated their stock in *Ms.* to the foundation, received back pay and contracts to be paid $100,000 a year for five years as consultants to the magazine. Some of the senior editors kept their jobs; the others received severance bonuses. There didn't seem to be any other way to keep the magazine going.

Not long after Yates and Summers took over, the main owner of Fairfax Publications died. The new leader decided to put *Ms.* up for sale again. Yates and Summers were dedicated to *Ms.* They bought the magazine but then had problems of their own. They sold it for the third time in two years, this time to Dale Lang, who also owned *Working Woman* and *Working Mother* magazines.

Before advertisers could be convinced that the new *Ms.* would be less controversial, the magazine took a bold stand in support of a woman's right to abortion. After the US Supreme Court ruled that states could restrict access to abortion, *Ms.* magazine defiantly declared "IT'S WAR" on the cover. Advertisers pulled back. The ad staff couldn't sell enough ads to cover the cost of publication.

It looked like *Ms.* was dead.

The new owner canceled the December 1989 magazine as well as the January Woman of the Year issue. Instead of publishing *Ms.*, Lang planned to have subscribers shift to either *Working Woman* or *Working Mother*. "That's not in the spirit of *Ms.*, at all," Steinem said. She told Lang that he was going to have to publish an advertisement-free, subscriber-supported version of *Ms.* or she would urge her subscribers to demand their money back. "The idea of having no ads at all is regarded as total folly by the magazine industry," Steinem said.

Lang looked at the numbers and decided to publish *Ms.* six times a year, without ads, and with a $40 annual subscription rate, almost three times more than the rate when the magazine accepted ads. They thought they would hold on to only 2 or 3 percent of their subscribers, but they had an almost 20 percent response rate. *Ms.* was relaunched in 1990 without advertising. In just nine months, the magazine was in the black.

"*Ms.* has found a new way of publishing by proving that readers will pay for what they really want," Steinem said.

. . . .

ONCE *MS.* WAS REBORN, the editors were free of worries about offending advertisers. The first noncommercial issue featured a bitter attack on the advertising industry written by Steinem.

Just as Steinem had realized in the late 1980s that the only way to save *Ms.* was to sell it, she realized ten years later that the only way to save the magazine was to buy it back. In 1998, *Ms.* was sold to Liberty Media for Women, a group of fourteen female investors, including Steinem. Finally, in 2001, the Feminist Majority Foundation, a women's action and research group, bought *Ms.*

The magazine reached middle age—it turned forty—in 2012. "The magazine, despite its flaws, provided so many words that had been missing, so many silences finally broken," Steinem said. "*Ms.* changed lives, changed attitudes, helped to create and change laws, policies, practices."

After a difficult decade, *Ms.* was back in feminist hands. The identity crisis was over—at least for the magazine.

Gloria Steinem in her New York City apartment,
November 2, 1990
[Barbara Alper/Getty Images]

CHAPTER 31

REFLECTION AND REVOLUTION

I, who had spent the previous dozen years working on external barriers to women's equality, had to admit there were internal ones, too.

—GLORIA STEINEM

It wasn't only *Ms.* magazine that went through a resurrection in the late 1980s and early 1990s. Gloria Steinem herself went through a period of personal reflection and reinvention, and, noting that we "write what we need to know," she completed her third book, *Revolution from Within: A Book of Self-Esteem.*

After decades of exhausting work for the women's movement,

Steinem found herself depleted. Her friends urged her to make a change in her lifestyle—to take better care of herself—and to seek the support of a therapist. Steinem knew they were right: She needed to take care of herself in the same way she took care of everyone else.

She began to slow down and say no more often. She started to eat better, sleep longer, and exercise more. She also decided to muster the courage to look into her past and begin to examine her feelings about her childhood traumas. She realized how the experiences of her past continued to affect her adult life in the present.

"I had been repeating the patterns of my childhood without recognizing them," Steinem wrote. She admitted that there were parts of her past that continued to haunt her, even though she had been running from them all her life. "In short, my childhood years—a part of my life I thought I had walled off—were still shaping the present as surely as a concealed magnet shapes metal dust."

· · · · · · · ·

WHAT SHE LEARNED from her therapy and extensive reading about self-esteem she wanted to share with other women. "The truth was that I had internalized society's *un*serious estimate of all that was female—including myself," Steinem wrote. "This was low self-esteem, not logic."

In 1992, she completed the book, which proved to be part recovery movement, part self-help advice, with Steinem's feminist outlooked mixed in. She included stories, which she called parables, about herself and other people she had researched or interviewed. The book wasn't about "self" alone; she wrote about how the messages we tell ourselves have an impact on the role we play in the feminist revolution. A woman won't stand up for herself if she doesn't think she deserves to be treated better than she has been.

Low self-esteem is a factor in other social problems. "Studies show that low self-esteem correlates with both prejudice and violence—that people who have a negative view of themselves also tend to view other people and the world negatively," Steinem wrote. In other words, the stakes are higher than simple self-fulfillment; healthy self-esteem can change the world.

As part of her research for the book, Steinem went through hypnosis to reimagine herself as a child. She remembered being in a small room with white walls dappled in summer sunlight. She was five or six years old, wearing a worn-out red bathing suit, lying on the cool sheets of a bed where she felt relaxed and "poured out like molasses."

Steinem smiled, feeling the child's lack of self-consciousness about her body and her physical exhaustion after a full day of play at Clark Lake. "It was odd to discover this untamed and spontaneous child: someone who existed *before* the terrifying years of living alone with my mother," Steinem wrote. Steinem lost touch with that confident young version of herself when she put up walls to protect herself from the difficult times she had with her mother when they were on their own.

Before this experience, Steinem thought that her childhood was behind her. "I thought I had built a brick wall between myself and my childhood," she said. "I valued those early years for making me an optimist (nothing could ever be that bad again) and a survivor (learning how to cope has its advantages). Then I put the memories and feelings behind me." But that wasn't true.

Steinem learned that she did not see herself as others saw her. She remembered feeling shocked the first time she saw herself on television. "There was this thin, pretty blondish woman of medium height who spoke in a boring monotone and, through lack of animation, seemed calm, even blasé in a New York way," she wrote. But that person on the screen wasn't the *real* Steinem. "What I felt *inside* was a plump brunette from Toledo, too tall and much too pudding-faced, with looks that might be pretty-on-a-good-day but were mostly very ordinary, and a voice that felt constantly on the verge of revealing some unacceptable emotion. I was amazed: Where had this woman on television come from?"

She had a distorted vision of herself. The time spent in therapy caused Steinem to ask herself a different question. She now asked: "Where did that woman in my mind come from?"

She had also begun to realize that these internal questions and perceptions had an important impact on political movements. "The idea for this book began a decade ago when even I, who had spent the previous dozen years working on external barriers to women's equality, had to admit there were internal ones, too," Steinem said. "Wherever I traveled, I saw women who were smart, courageous, and valuable, who didn't *think* they were smart, courageous, or valuable—and this was true not only for women who were poor or otherwise doubly discriminated against, but for supposedly privileged and powerful women, too."

• • • • • • • •

REVOLUTION FROM WITHIN used a lot of language from the recovery movement, which was popular at the time. She encouraged the women and men reading the book to get to know their "inner child" and to reparent that person in order to heal and find their true selves. This wasn't simply a study of self and self-esteem; Steinem saw this internal quest as a way of empowering women to become stronger and more confident in their external lives as well.

The book wasn't easy to write. In the first draft, Steinem wrote a manuscript that didn't include her own experiences. One of her manuscript reviewers said, "I don't know how to tell you this—but I think you have a self-esteem problem. You forgot to put yourself in." Steinem needed to include more personal reflection in the work.

"Why would anyone be interested in my experiences?" Steinem asked. She realized the reviewer was right, so she rewrote the manuscript and added more personal anecdotes.

Readers reported that they particularly appreciated Steinem's personal stories. Women identified with Steinem when she shared her fears and failures, and they found solace and inspiration in learning that she had been able to get through her difficulties. After all, Steinem lived in the same sexist world with the same cultural messages as other women, and if she had transcended some of these toxic messages, then they could, too.

For example, in the essay "The Body in Our Minds," Steinem wrote about her lifelong struggle with her weight. "I'm still trying to thread a path between outside images and inner self, and this is just a progress report," Steinem wrote. "For instance: I'm still suspicious of the degree to which I make choices that society rewards."

She acknowledged that she had worked her entire life to remain thin. She realized that her obsession about her weight was linked to her childhood. Where did the plump, vulnerable girl in her head come from? Why did she stand stoop-shouldered as a girl? Why did she hide behind a screen of hair and huge glasses as an adult? Only after considering these questions did Steinem begin to change.

Steinem also worried that she had inherited her father's genetic predisposition to gain weight; he weighed more than three hundred pounds. "I loved him for his sense of adventure, for looking after me when I was very little and my mother could not, and for so much more; yet I was often ashamed of his huge size," Steinem wrote.

Her father's weight problem became Steinem's weight problem. "I am his daughter," she wrote. "Like a recovering alcoholic, I'm a foodaholic who can't keep food in the house." Steinem never felt like the thin woman reflected when she looked in a mirror. "I am not a thin woman, I'm a fat woman who's not fat at the moment." These factors may have contributed to her body-image issues, but she acknowledges that her body-image issues were further complicated because she also wanted society's approval for being thin.

• • • • • • • •

EVEN THOUGH THE book became a bestseller, it did not receive the reception that Steinem had hoped for. Many critics called *Revolution from Within* Steinem's midlife crisis and joked that she couldn't possibly have self-esteem problems. *Newsweek* dismissed the book as a "squishy exercise in feeling better." Reviewers didn't look at self-esteem as a serious subject. Steinem wanted respect for her ideas, especially since she had shared so much of herself in this work. "I began to wonder if I really had written what I thought I had written," Steinem said.

Still, her readers responded positively to the book and to Steinem's willingness to share that she had the same experiences and problems as other women. "If I wasn't immune, either, they said in various ways, then perhaps they were not personally at fault," Steinem wrote. Using her book as a guide, women could start the revolution within and then expand it to the broader world. "There really was a sexual caste system at work, and together, we could change it."

SPECIAL!
COLLECTORS ISSUE

AFGHAN WOMEN · A FEMINIST FAMILY TREE

Ms.

VOLUME XII NUMBER 2 · SPRING 2002 · U.S. $5.95 CANADA $6.95

the best of
30 years

Reporting
Rebelling &
Truth-telling
Plus Updates:
Moving into the Future

DISPLAY UNTIL JUNE 24

21>

0 71896 46962 2

Ms. magazine cover, spring 2002
[*Ms.* magazine/Wikimedia Commons]

CHAPTER 32

AGING

More and more, there is only the full, glorious, alive-in-the-moment, don't-give-a-damn yet caring-for-everything sense of the now.

—GLORIA STEINEM

When Gloria Steinem turned fifty, a friend sent her a photograph of an old Chinese woman, which she posted on her kitchen wall. "She was in a park in the early morning doing tai chi and singing opera," Steinem said. "This woman had lots of wrinkles, a gorgeous, beatific smile, and a lilac kerchief. She looked happy, wise, mischievous, and peaceful. She was absolutely beautiful. The moment I saw her I felt, 'This is the person I want to grow into.'"

Just a few weeks before, she had planned to defy expectations; she said she refused to grow old. "I was going to live exactly as I always had—and make a virtue of it," she said. Her attitude was: "The world could use a pioneer dirty old lady."

Steinem wanted to both embrace and defy the idea of growing older. This was nothing new; she always had a complex relationship with aging and youth. As a teen, she lied about her age to be old enough to tap-dance in clubs; as a young woman, she lied about her age to be young enough to audition as a Playboy Bunny for a magazine article. People have typically thought Steinem was younger than her true age, and often she didn't bother to correct them.

For Steinem, aging wasn't measured by the traditional markers of marriage, parenthood, and work that ends in retirement. "The central years of adulthood seemed as if they could stretch on forever," she said. "If I was 'old' when I was younger, and, according to work and lifestyle, 'young' when I was old, how relevant could aging be?"

Steinem has reflected openly about her feelings regarding growing older. In her 1994 book *Moving Beyond Words*, she wrote an essay titled "Doing Sixty." Steinem said that the older she got, the freer she felt. "I've come to realize the pleasures of being a nothing-to-lose, take-no-shit older woman, of looking at what once seemed to be outer limits but turned out to be just road signs," Steinem wrote. "I'm looking forward to trading moderation for excess, defiance for openness, and planning for the unknown . . . More and more, there is only the full, glorious, alive-in-the-moment, don't-give-a-damn yet caring-for-everything sense of the right now."

In the essay, Steinem explored the link between growing older and building a home for herself. "I used to walk around the streets of New York looking in lighted windows, thinking, *Everybody has a family but me*," Steinem wrote. "*Everybody has a home.* I hadn't made my own home. You have to do that for yourself, but it was a lot of years before I did."

She had an apartment, but she hadn't *nested*. She had never bothered to create a home, a place of her own where she felt she belonged. "Home is a symbol of the self," Steinem said. "Caring for a home is caring for one's self."

In the essay, Steinem revealed the depth of her feelings of vulnerability. "I always thought of myself as a survivor. But I was very frightened and depressed by the idea of ending up, in a sense, where I began," she wrote. "That's the price of changing a lot in your life."

Throughout her life, Steinem had yearned for a family, the connection to people she could call her own. "For many years I was jealous of people with families. And so part of my attraction to friends, both men and women, was their families. I was, in a sense, joining their families." In time, she created her own family, her "chosen family," a group of friends and ex-lovers she cared about. Writer Alice Walker and Cherokee leader Wilma Mankiller became some of her closest friends, women she named her "sisters of the heart."

Walker became a close friend after becoming a writer at *Ms.*

Steinem always appreciated Walker's instincts, describing her as a "moral compass." She trusted Walker's heart, often testing her true feelings by discussing issues with her dear friend. "Alice Walker is someone in my life who helps me know what's true to my inner voice," Steinem said. "I think, could I tell this to Alice Walker? Because she's a very shit-free person."

Steinem never regretted her decision not to have children. She may not have given birth to the young women she cared about, but the women she mentored became her "surrogate daughters." She redefined family, rejecting marriage and childbirth in favor of serial monogamy and building relationships with people she chose to love.

One of Steinem's surrogate daughters is Rebecca Walker, Alice Walker's daughter and Steinem's goddaughter. Rebecca stayed with Steinem most summers after college, and she became a contributing editor at *Ms.* "She was my champion, my support," said Rebecca. Steinem modeled how to disagree with people respectfully. Rebecca admired how Steinem would remain calm and speak lovingly with other people, even when they had different points of view. "I think her approach really allowed them to hear," Rebecca said, noting that Steinem's patient approach would reverberate in a way that screaming didn't. "I also felt that it created a lot more room for humanity, that kind of civility, and so I started to take that into my own life."

In the 1990s, Steinem also started to make a home that reflected who she was. She had lived in the same Upper East Side brownstone since the late 1960s. She used money she received from a book deal to buy the apartment below hers, and she started renovations, turning two rooms into a study and a bedroom. Homemaking didn't come easily to her. Steinem once lived in an apartment for four years before she discovered that the oven was broken, and she kept the refrigerator empty most of the time because she feared that in a moment of weakness she would binge-eat all the food she had in the house. This time, Steinem consciously decided to set up her house the way she wanted it. She unpacked all the boxes, put up curtains, and chose throw pillows that made her feel at home. She wanted to be active and engaged with the world outside, but she wanted to have a place she could call her own to come home to at the end of the day.

• • • • • • • •

FOR STEINEM'S SIXTY-FIFTH BIRTHDAY, several friends took her to Jezebel, a New Orleans–style restaurant in Manhattan. When they arrived, 135 guests welcomed her for a surprise party. In her honor, they had created a Gloria's Future Fund at the Ms. Foundation, and they already had more than two million dollars in pledges. Steinem would have the privilege of using the money to support causes she considered worthy.

Congresswoman Bella Abzug attended the party and paid tribute to Steinem. "She's crystallized the emotions and the yearnings of our entire gender," Abzug said. "She's served as our most vivid expression of our hopes and demands. She's our pen and our tongue and our heart. She's Elizabeth Cady Stanton and Susan B. Anthony and Emma Goldman all rolled up into one—and she still doesn't gain any weight."

At the party, the editors of *Ms.* gave Steinem a personalized cover of *Ms.* magazine. It featured a photograph of Steinem with teasers promising "Ten Surefire Tips for Meeting Deadlines," "Stories for Free Children: My Inner Child," and a special pullout, "Steinem in the Year 2035: This Is What 101 Looks Like."

Steinem approached her sixty-fifth and other landmark birthdays with a sense of curiosity and humor. She called herself a hardy perennial, repotted again and again to bloom many times. More than quips, Steinem has developed a strategy to stay younger in spirit. She said that "newness stretches out our experience of time, but familiarity shortens it." She developed her own twist on Einstein's Theory of Relativity: "If time is relative, doing new things actually makes us feel we've lived a longer life." These new experiences also give her life more meaning. Steinem said that when she looks back at her life, she does so with gratitude. "Each day, I thought the next couldn't possibly be more intense and satisfying—and then it was."

Throughout her life, Steinem always embraced new paths and new ideas. She also allowed herself permission to change her mind, even about issues that no one ever thought she would reconsider—such as marriage.

Gloria Steinem and her husband, David Bale, in New York City, 2001
[Robin Platzer/Getty Images]

CHAPTER 33

MARRIAGE

I couldn't imagine why I would get married. I was happy as I was.

— GLORIA STEINEM

Gloria Steinem didn't expect to marry. She had been in a number of committed relationships and had considered marriage several times in her life, but each time she decided not to say "I do."

And then she changed her mind.

On September 3, 2000, at age sixty-six, Steinem married David

Bale, a South African–born anti-apartheid and animal-rights activist, businessman, and father of four grown children. (His son is Academy Award–winning actor Christian Bale.) Bale ran a commuter airline in England and sat on the board of directors of the Ark Trust, an animal rights group, as well as the Dian Fossey Gorilla Fund International.

The couple met at a fund-raising benefit for Voters for Choice, a pro-choice political action committee organized by Steinem. Bale was smitten. "Those amazing brown eyes just looking back at you, the intelligence, the warmth, the humor. I was completely in love," said Bale, who had been married twice before. Bale said he used to encourage other people to read Steinem's work, saying, "Read this woman. She's a prophet."

Steinem downplayed the focus on marriage. "We're calling it a 'partnership,'" she said. Instead of "husband" and "wife," they called each other "the friend I married."

When asked why she changed her mind about getting married, Steinem said, "I did not change; the idea of marriage did." So did the laws. "Thirty years of the women's movement had changed the marriage laws and made an equal marriage possible," she said.

Steinem said that her decision to marry had nothing to do with a change in her attitude toward feminism. "I hope this proves what feminists have always said—that feminism is about the ability to choose what's right at each time of our lives," Steinem said.

The couple chose a Cherokee wedding ceremony, which was performed at dawn in Stilwell, Oklahoma, by Steinem's friend Wilma Mankiller, a former chief of the Cherokee Nation, and her husband, Charlie Soap, a Cherokee spiritual leader. Steinem dressed in jeans and a T-shirt. Bale wore black jeans and a black shirt. She was sixty-six years old; Bale was fifty-nine. They exchanged ninety-five-cent beaded rings.

"There was no use of words like *husband* and *wife*, that kind of nonsense," said David Bale. A judge did legalize the marriage.

• • • • • • • •

FOR DECADES, Steinem didn't see the need to get married, at least not for her. "I couldn't imagine why I would get married," Steinem said. "I was happy as I was." She said that, in her experience, "marriage felt like a restriction, not an enlargement."

She reconsidered the issue when she and Bale were spending time together in California. They talked about marriage, but she wasn't sure. She called Mankiller and asked for advice on whether to rethink her position on marriage. The next day they started planning the wedding.

"Being married is like having somebody permanently in your corner," Steinem said. "It feels limitless, not limited."

In later interviews, Steinem also acknowledged that one of the reasons she married Bale was because of his immigration status; he was facing deportation for overstaying his visa. "We wouldn't have got married if he hadn't needed a visa," Steinem later said. "We loved each other, we wanted to be together, but we wouldn't have legally married if it hadn't been that he still had a British passport."

Steinem didn't mention the immigration issue when Barbara Walters interviewed her about her decision to marry. In the interview, Walters reminded Steinem that she had once said: "You become a semi-nonperson when you get married. The surest way to be alone is to get married."

"Yeah, well, I think that's often true," Steinem replied. "But to be against unequal marriage is not the same thing as being against marriage. I was a happy single person for fifty years."

Walters asked Steinem why she didn't just live with Bale. "Because we both felt that we wanted to be responsible for each other." She ended the interview by saying, "If we compete about anything it's who's going to take care of the other one because we both grew up being caretakers."

As it turned out, Steinem was the one called on to be a caretaker. Not long after that interview, Bale was diagnosed with brain cancer. Steinem stayed by his side until he died in December 2003 at age sixty-two of a brain lymphoma. "David went through the world with few possessions and great empathy for all living things," Steinem said in a press statement at the time of Bale's death. "He had the greatest heart of anyone I've ever known."

Steinem said that caring for Bale during his last year of life proved to be therapeutic for her. Bale "needed someone to help him out of life, and I needed someone to force me to live in the present." The process also helped Steinem face her fears about entrapment related to her experiences of caring for her mother when she was a young girl.

"It was terrible, terrible, the two years of his illness and afterward," Steinem said. "But, looking back, though I don't believe anything to be preordained . . . there was a purpose. His purpose in my life was, as my friends all said, to make me feel deeply, and to live in the present. Because I live in the future. My purpose was to give him something that he hadn't had. . . . And then . . . I ushered him out of life. His kids were there, and they were wonderful, but a contemporary is a different thing. In a way, he taught me about dying."

Steinem stayed by Bale's side until he died. "It was actually very good for me," she said. "It was as though life had given me a chance for a redo. Being an adult taking care of an adult is very different than being a child doing it." In her childhood, Steinem was forced to care for her mentally ill mother because there was no one else to do it. This time, she chose to nurture and support her loved one from a position of strength and maturity.

"Despite the shortness, despite the suffering of watching him suffer, I would not have missed or changed a thing," Steinem wrote. "We both planted and grew in years that are supposed to be only those of harvest. He pushed and nudged and inspired and loved me out of old ruts and patterns and choices."

As her seventieth birthday approached, Steinem was once again single, only this time, she was a widow.

Gloria Steinem campaigning for Hillary Clinton. September 2016.
[Gage Skidmore/ Wikimedia Commons]

CHAPTER 34

BEYOND

I'm using my torch to light other torches.

— GLORIA STEINEM

G loria Steinem didn't expect to have her life defined by the women's movement. "In my first days of feminism, I thought I would do this ('this' being feminism) for a few years and then turn to my real life (what my 'real life' might be, I do not know)," Steinem wrote in *Outrageous Acts and Everyday Rebellions*. "But like so many others now and in movements past, I've learned that this is not something we care about for a year or two or three. We are in it for life—and for our lives."

There's no doubt that Steinem's life was shaped by her belief in the equality of women and men. She considered—and rejected—the life of wife and mother, choosing instead to remain unmarried for most of her life and to devote much of her creative energy and career to working within the women's movement. Her choice not to marry and have children as a young woman gave Steinem more available time and energy to work on feminist causes. Her lack of family commitments and obligations also set her free to be herself, without being accused of emasculating her husband or neglecting her children. In addition, as a single woman, many people considered her less threatening; without a man, she was dismissed as abnormal, unnatural, maybe even less than fully female.

Even though she did not have a traditional family, Steinem needed to be needed. "Even if we're no longer trying to surgically transplant our egos into the body of a husband or children, we still may be overly dependent on being needed—by coworkers and bosses, lover and friends, even by the very movements that were intended to free us of all that," Steinem wrote.

Steinem earned a reputation for being generous with her time and resources. She supported the people and causes she cared about, and she freely shared her money and access to power when other activists needed a hand. In fact, some feminists considered Steinem's selfless and saintly behavior a problem for a feminist icon. "To me, the idea that she's completely selfless, that she'll do anything, is a put-down . . . I'm not interested in a selfless leader," said feminist Marie C. Wilson. "I got into this movement because I wanted to have a self."

In time, Steinem learned to set boundaries so that she would not be consumed by the demands and needs of other people. "I'd been submerging myself, not in the traditional needs of husband and children, true, but in the needs of others nonetheless," she said. "Having been bred by class and gender to know what other people wanted and needed better than I knew what I did, I had turned all my antennae outward."

Steinem developed what she called the women's version of the golden rule: "The need to treat ourselves as well as we treat others." It's not easy, especially when our culture reinforces the idea that women are supposed to be nurturing caregivers. "I have yet to meet a woman who has completely kicked the habit of leading a derived life that depends more on her sense of others than her sense of herself," she wrote.

• • • • • • • •

GROWING OLDER HAS made Steinem freer. "Fifty was hardest for me, because it's the end of the center of life, especially a gendered center of life," Steinem said. "But by the time I got to be sixty, it was like a new world. Society has given up [on older women] because it's all about having or raising children, really, and by sixty, society doesn't care that much, so you're free. Seventy was certainly about mortality. And eighty even more so."

But growing older didn't slow Steinem down. She continued making a difference in her forties, fifties, sixties, seventies, and eighties.

At age forty, in 1974, she founded the Coalition of Labor Union Women, a group of more than sixty national and international trade unions.

At age forty-four, in 1978, she cofounded Women Against Pornography, a feminist antipornography group; in the mid-1990s the group evolved into the Coalition Against Trafficking in Women.

At age forty-five, in 1979, she cofounded Voters for Choice, a pro-choice political-action committee.

At age fifty-eight, in 1992, Steinem founded Choice USA, a youth-led reproductive rights organization; in 2014, the organization changed its name to URGE: Unite for Reproductive and Gender Equity.

At age fifty-nine, in 1993, she was executive producer for the Lifetime movie *Better Off Dead*, a movie about abortion and the death penalty. The same year, she also coproduced the Emmy Award–winning HBO movie *Multiple Personalities: The Search for Deadly Memories*.

At seventy, in 2004, she cofounded the Women's Media Center, which promotes the accurate portrayal of female perspectives in the media.

At seventy-seven, in 2011, she was the subject of the HBO documentary *Gloria: In Her Own Words*.

At seventy-nine, in 2013, she advised the production of *Lovelace*, a feature film about the life of porn star Linda "Lovelace" Boreman. That year, she was also one of the subjects in the PBS series *Makers: Women Who Make America*.

At age eighty-one, in 2015, Steinem joined thirty-one peace

activists from thirteen countries to fly to North Korea on a peace mission that involved crossing the demilitarized zone, the DMZ.

At age eighty-two, in 2016, she was executive producer of *Woman with Gloria Steinem*, a Viceland documentary television series about women around the world.

At age eighty-three, in 2017, she took the stage as the honorary cochair of the Women's March on Washington, held the day after Donald Trump's presidential inauguration. The event—the largest single-day protest in United States history—included about five hundred thousand people in Washington, as well as three to five million in more than six hundred events that took place across the country and around the world. "This is an outpouring of energy and true democracy like I have never seen in my very long life," said Steinem.

At age eighty-four, in 2018, the play *Gloria: A Life* opened at the Daryl Roth Theatre off Broadway in New York City. The play consists of a series of short scenes, portraying experiences in Steinem's life. The second act is a twenty-minute talking circle in which audience members are invited to respond to what they've seen and heard. The play summarizes the highlights of Steinem's life, a collection of her greatest hits, but it ends with ellipses . . . as if the story isn't finished, because the women's movement isn't finished—and neither is Steinem.

"I hope to live to one hundred," Steinem said. "There is so much to do."

• • • • • • • •

OVER THE DECADES, Steinem has traveled and spoken on college campuses and other forums throughout the country. She estimates that for a period of at least twenty years, she never went more than a week without being on an airplane. Constantly in motion—not restless motion, but intentional motion—movement from place to place to speak and inspire and listen.

Steinem has remained active in politics, although she stopped officially joining political campaigns years ago. She prefers to remain an independent voice so that she can maintain the freedom to speak out, regardless of a particular candidate's position on an issue. "If you work on a campaign, anything you say reflects on your candidate, and I want—no, I need—to be free to disagree," Steinem said.

In recent years, Steinem has spoken out against gun violence, which she sees as an inevitable consequence of patriarchy. She has argued that when children die at the hands of white men with guns, the crime is rarely blamed on white men *or* guns. Instead, *mental-health issues* become the scapegoat. Steinem supports the need for better mental-health care, but for those who blame mass shootings on mental health, Steinem has a response: "In that case, masculinity is a mental illness."

"Guns are related to masculinity," she said. She notes that white men who feel powerless are the most likely to misuse guns. "They are exactly the group of people who are most likely to have been told by society that they have a right to dominate others," she said. "And when they are not able to dominate others, then they kill in order to prove their power."

In many cases, men who commit violent acts with guns also physically abuse women. "Men who are guilty of domestic violence are way more likely to own guns than men who are not," Steinem says. "These things are related." In Steinem's view, feminism could rebalance the world order in a way that would have a positive impact on all aspects of society, including gun violence.

. . . .

ONE OF THE more difficult parts of growing older has been saying goodbye to loved ones. In addition to outliving her parents, her sister (who died in 2007), and her husband, Steinem also watched her dear friend Wilma Mankiller die in 2010. "We were a chosen family," Steinem said of Mankiller, who suffered from a number of health problems during her life but ultimately died of pancreatic cancer.

Steinem had supported Mankiller during chemotherapy for an earlier cancer. She drove her friend to the hospital for treatment and spent the summer with her watching every episode of *Prime Suspect*, a British television program starring Helen Mirren as a feisty feminist police detective. During their time together, Steinem learned that Mankiller hoped to preserve what she called the Way, a belief that the earth was a living organism and that someday the human experiment would end and the world would be reborn.

"This worldview has more layers than I know," Steinem said, "but it seems to start with a circle in which all living things are related." The goal is balance, not dominance.

When Mankiller was diagnosed with advanced pancreatic cancer, there was little that could be done to slow the progression of the disease. Steinem stayed with Mankiller, trying to offer comfort and connection as long as possible. There was no final goodbye. "Wilma just seemed to pull away from us, like an ocean tide receding from all of us left standing on the beach," Steinem wrote.

Still, the moment of death felt momentous. "The moment after is utterly different from the moment before," Steinem wrote. "Now I understand why people believe the soul departs with the last breath. Everything looks the same, yet everything is different."

They had been so close that for years after Mankiller's death, Steinem continued to reach for her phone to call her friend, only to remember that she was gone. "I once asked Wilma if one day my ashes could be with hers, and she said yes," Steinem said. Mankiller's ashes were scattered on the banks of the spring where the medicinal herbs grow on the family's land on Mankiller Flats, the family homestead in rural Oklahoma. Someday Steinem may join her there.

• • • • • • • •

STEINEM HAS MADE plans to support the women's movement, even after she is gone. Her birthday and other celebrations have been used as an excuse to raise money for feminist causes, and she has said, "My funeral will be a fund-raiser." She has arranged so that when she dies her New York City brownstone will become a halfway house for feminists, a place for those interested in the women's movement to gather and write and organize. "I don't plan to die," she said. "I'll be at home, with those women."

Steinem has dedicated her life—and her afterlife—to promoting feminism, building equality between women and men, and making the world more just. She has done what she can, where she can, to advocate for what is right and equitable.

"People are always asking me, 'Who will you pass the torch to?'" Steinem said. "The question makes me angry. There is no one torch—there are many torches—and I'm using my torch to light other torches."

Steinem has argued throughout her life that she is not and never has been the torch or the voice or the face of the women's movement. Like other big concepts—such as equality and justice and fairness—feminism is a broad and vibrant idea, one that is deceptively simple to explain and exquisitely hard to implement, one that must be spread not by a single individual but from person to person, heart to heart, generation to generation, reader to reader. While Steinem's life may inspire us, she is not the epicenter of the women's movement; instead, she would argue, every woman is the center of her own experience.

THE MS. FOUNDATION

GLORIA STEINEM AND the founders of *Ms.* wanted to do more than simply publish a magazine. They wanted to change women's lives by supporting organizations and programs that helped women with employment, domestic abuse, reproductive health, and other issues. To achieve that goal, in 1972, *Ms.* magazine established the nonprofit Ms. Foundation for Women.

The Ms. Foundation published a number of books, including *The Ms. Guide to a Woman's Health* and *The First Ms. Reader*, an anthology. Their most successful project was the 1972 *Free to Be . . . You and Me,* a recording of nonsexist songs and skits for children, performed by various actors and singers. It was also turned into a book and an Emmy Award–winning television special in 1974.

The foundation took the lead on dealing with controversial issues. In 1976, they became the first national foundation to give money to shelters for women suffering from domestic violence. The following year, they funded a project to defend lesbian mothers threatened with losing custody of their children.

One of the best-known projects started by the Ms. Foundation is Take Our Daughters to Work Day, which began in 1992. The goal of the project was to introduce girls to a broad range of job opportunities, but the program met with some resistance. Critics claim it discriminates against boys. A religious group in Arkansas started a "Take Your Daughter Home" day to encourage girls to stay home and learn cooking and other domestic skills.

When asked if Take Our Daughters to Work Day is unfair to boys, Steinem usually quotes Congresswoman Eleanor Holmes Norton, who said, "There's no Take Our Sons to Work Day for the same reason there's no White History Month."

The foundation sometimes had to do some soul-searching to decide whether to accept certain donations. In 1982 the foundation returned about $10,000 in donations from the Playboy Foundation. They initially took the money so that they could use it to support their programs, but Playboy began to publicize the fact that it was supporting women. The foundation refused to be used in the Playboy public relations campaign, so it gave back the money.

TIMELINE OF GLORIA STEINEM'S LIFE

1934: Gloria Marie Steinem is born in Toledo, Ohio, on March 25.

1944: Steinem's parents, Ruth and Leo Steinem, divorce.

1951: Steinem moves to Washington, DC, to live with her sister, Susanne.

1956: Steinem graduates from Smith College on June 3.

1957: Steinem has an abortion in England, then travels to India on a fellowship and stays for two years.

1959: Steinem works for the Independent Research Service, unaware that the organization receives funding from the Central Intelligence Agency.

1960: Steinem moves to New York City and works as a freelance writer.

1961: Steinem's father, Leo Steinem, dies in an automobile accident in California.

1961: Steinem helps organize Women Strike for Peace to campaign for a nuclear-test ban.

1968: Steinem works with the United Farm Workers on the grape boycott.

1969: Steinem identifies as a feminist after covering a rally by the radical feminist group the Redstockings.

1970: Steinem wins the Penney-Missouri Journalism Award and begins lecturing on feminist issues.

1971: Steinem cofounds the National Women's Political Caucus, with Bella Abzug, Shirley Chisholm, Betty Friedan, and others.

1971: The *Ms.* magazine preview issue appears as an insert in *New York* magazine's December issue.

1972: Steinem cofounds *Ms.* magazine. First regular issue is on newsstands in July.

1972: Steinem speaks for the National Women's Political Caucus at the Democratic Presidential Convention.

1977: Steinem serves on the commission for the National Women's Conference in Houston, which attracts twenty thousand delegates who debate a twenty-six-plank National Plan of Action.

1983: Steinem publishes *Outrageous Acts and Everyday Rebellions*.

1986: Steinem is diagnosed with breast cancer.

1988: Ms. Foundation creates the Gloria Award for feminist accomplishment.

1992: Steinem publishes *Revolution from Within: A Book of Self-Esteem*.

1992: Ms. Foundation launches Take Our Daughters to Work Day.

1993: Steinem is inducted into the National Women's Hall of Fame.

1994: Steinem publishes *Moving Beyond Words*.

2000: Steinem marries activist David Bale on September 3.

2003: David Bale dies in December.

2013: Barack Obama awards Steinem the Presidential Medal of Freedom.

2014: Rutgers University endows a chair in media, culture, and feminist studies in Steinem's honor.

2014: Steinem receives the Eleanor Roosevelt Val-Kill Medal Award.

2017: Ms. Magazine Way is dedicated at the intersection of Thirty-Second Street and Third Avenue in New York City.

2018: The play *Gloria: A Life* opens at the Daryl Roth Theatre in New York City.

Suffragists in Washington, DC, 1913
[Library of Congress]

Margaret Sanger [Library of Congress]

Anita Hill [Library of Congress]

Sandra Day O'Connor [Library of
Congress]

TIMELINE OF AMERICAN FEMINISM

FIRST-WAVE FEMINISM

The period of feminist activity from the mid-nineteenth century to the early twentieth century, focusing primarily on voting rights and property rights.

1848: The first women's rights convention held in Seneca Falls, New York.

1866: Congress passes the Fourteenth Amendment, which defines *citizens* and *voters* as male.

1869: The territory of Wyoming passes the first women's suffrage law, granting women the right to vote and hold office.

1869: Iowa resident Arabella Mansfield becomes the first female lawyer.

1869: Susan B. Anthony and Elizabeth Cady Stanton found the National Woman Suffrage Association to work for a constitutional amendment to give women the right to vote.

1869: Lucy Stone and Henry Blackwell and others form the American Woman Suffrage Association to work for voting rights for women on a state-by-state basis.

1872: Victoria Woodhull becomes the first female presidential candidate, nominated by the National Radical Reformers.

1890: Wyoming becomes a state, making it the first to grant women the right to vote.

1890: The National Woman Suffrage Association and the American Woman Suffrage Association merge to form the National American Woman Suffrage Association.

1896: The National Association of Colored Women becomes an umbrella organization for more than one hundred African American women's clubs.

1913: Alice Paul and Lucy Burns form the Congressional Union to work toward passage of a federal amendment to give women the right to vote.

1916: Jeannette Rankin of Montana becomes the first woman elected to Congress.

1916: Margaret Sanger opens the first US birth control clinic in Brooklyn, New York.

1917: Alice Paul and the Congressional Union picket the White House and practice civil disobedience to gain support of a women's suffrage amendment.

1919: The women's suffrage amendment, originally written by Susan B. Anthony and introduced to Congress in 1878, is passed by Congress and sent to the states for ratification.

1920: The ratification of the Nineteenth Amendment to the Constitution grants women the right to vote.

1921: Margaret Sanger founds the American Birth Control League, which becomes Planned Parenthood Federation of America in 1942.

1923: The first version of the Equal Rights Amendment is introduced to Congress.

1925: Congress grants American Indians the right to vote.

1932: Hattie Wyatt Caraway of Arkansas becomes the first female elected to the US Senate.

SECOND-WAVE FEMINISM

The period of feminist activity from the early 1960s to the early 1980s, focusing on legal issues about workplace equality, reproductive rights, sexuality, and violence against women.

1961: President John F. Kennedy establishes the President's Commission on the Status of Women with Eleanor Roosevelt as chairwoman; the report documents discrimination against women in the workplace and recommends improvements.

1961: The Food and Drug Administration approves oral contraceptives ("the pill").

1963: Betty Friedan publishes *The Feminine Mystique.*

1963: Congress passes the Equal Pay Act, promising equal pay for the same work, regardless of sex, race, religion, or national origin of the worker.

1964: Title VII of the Civil Rights Act prohibits discrimination in employment on the basis of sex and race; it establishes the Equal Employment Opportunity Commission to investigate complaints.

1965: The Supreme Court establishes the right of married couples to use contraception.

1966: Betty Friedan and other feminists form the National Organization for Women.

1968: Women protest the Miss America pageant in Atlantic City in the first national feminist protest since suffrage.

1970: Fifty thousand women march down Fifth Avenue in New York City, on August 26, in celebration of the fiftieth anniversary of women's suffrage.

1971: *Ms.* Magazine is published; it begins regular publication in 1972.

1971: National Women's Political Caucus is formed to increase female participation in politics.

1972: Title IX of the Education Amendments prohibits sexual discrimination in education.

1972: The Equal Rights Amendment is passed by Congress and sent to the states for ratification; it dies in 1982 when it fails to be ratified by the minimum of thirty-eight states.

1973: In *Roe v. Wade*, the US Supreme Court in a 7–2 decision declares that the Constitution protects a woman's right to choose abortion.

1974: Congress passes laws against housing and credit discrimination against women, giving women the right to rent apartments and get credit cards without a male cosigner.

1975: The Supreme Court denies the states' right to exclude women from juries.

1976: The first marital rape law is enacted in Nebraska, making it illegal for a husband to rape his wife.

1978: The Pregnancy Discrimination Act bans employment discrimination against pregnant women.

1980: Paula Hawkins of Florida becomes the first woman to be elected to the US Senate without following her husband or father to the job.

1981: Sandra Day O'Connor becomes the first woman to serve on the US Supreme Court.

1981: In England, Lady Diana Spencer omits the vow to "obey" her husband when she marries Prince Charles.

1982: The ERA fails to be ratified.

1983: Dr. Sally Ride becomes the first female astronaut, flying on the Space Shuttle *Challenger*.

1984: Geraldine Ferraro becomes the first vice presidential nominee by a major political party when Democratic presidential nominee Walter Mondale chooses her as his running mate.

1985: EMILY's List is founded to support the election of Democratic, pro-choice women to office.

1989: The Supreme Court supports the rights of states to deny public funding for abortions and to prohibit public hospitals from performing abortions.

THIRD-WAVE FEMINISM

The period of feminist activity from the early 1990s to the 2010s, when Generation Xers (those born in the 1960s and 1970s who grew up with a greater expectation of equality) reframed feminism with a focus on individualism and diversity.

1989: Kimberlé Williams Crenshaw introduces the concept of *intersectionality* to describe the idea that women face layers of oppression caused by gender, race, class, and sexual orientation.

1991: Anita Hill testifies before the Senate Judiciary Committee that Supreme Court Justice nominee Clarence Thomas sexually harassed her.

1991: Riot grrrl movement begins in Olympia, Washington, and Washington, DC.

1992: Take Our Daughters to Work Day established; the first event took place on April 22, 1993.

1993: Janet Reno becomes the first female attorney general of the United States.

1994: The Violence Against Women Act increases funding for prosecution of violent crimes against women and requires restitution from those convicted.

1997: Madeleine Albright becomes the first female secretary of state of the United States.

2005: Women's Media Center is formed to promote healthy portrayals of females in the media.

2007: US Representative Nancy Pelosi (Democrat, California) becomes the first female speaker of the House.

FOURTH-WAVE FEMINISM

A period of feminism that began around 2012, focusing on the use of the internet and social media to empower women and to increase the representation of women and marginalized groups in politics and business.

2012: The Everyday Sexism Project gives women a place to report sexist encounters.

2013: The US military removes a ban against women serving in combat positions.

2014: President Obama launches the White House Task Force to Protect Students from Sexual Assault.

2014: Gamergate examines sexual harassment of female video-game developers.

2016: Hillary Clinton becomes the first woman to be nominated for president by a major political party.

2017: The day after the inauguration of President Donald Trump, between three and five million Americans participate in marches across the country to advocate for policies protecting human rights and women's rights; it was the largest single-day protest in US history.

2017: The #MeToo campaign begins in response to Harvey Weinstein abuse allegations.

2018: The Time's Up movement against sexual harassment is founded by Hollywood celebrities.

Shirley Chisholm
[Library of Congress]

Fannie Lou Hamer
[Library of Congress]

Eleanor Norton
[Congress.gov]

PARTNERS IN JUSTICE

GLORIA STEINEM PRACTICED intersectional feminism back in the 1970s, years before activists had coined the expression. She recognized the connections between the discrimination faced by women and the discrimination faced by people of color. Steinem believed that by working together, a unified social movement combining feminists and civil rights activists could be more powerful than either group would be on its own.

Intersectional feminism is a theory introduced by lawyer, civil rights advocate, and scholar Kimberlé Crenshaw, a professor at UCLA School of Law and Columbia Law School. The theory examines the overlapping oppression and discrimination faced by women based on gender, race, sexuality, socioeconomic position, physical ability, and other social identities.

In her career as a feminist and a civil rights activist, Steinem worked with a number of important African American women, including Shirley Chisholm, Jane Galvin-Lewis, Fannie Lou Hamer, Dorothy Pitman Hughes, Florynce "Flo" Kennedy, Eleanor Holmes Norton, and Margaret Sloan-Hunter. Steinem recognized that African American women experience "the double discrimination of sex and race—not only in the mainstream but also by race in the women's movement, and by sex in the Black power movement." She advocated for racial and class diversity in the women's movement throughout her years as an activist.

Bella Abzug
[Library of Congress]

Wilma Mankiller
[Phil Konstantin/ Flickr]

Alice Walker with Gloria Steinem
[*Ms.* magazine/Wikimedia Commons]

WHO'S WHO: A PAGE FROM GLORIA STEINEM'S SCRAPBOOK

BELLA ABZUG: Feminist lawyer, social activist, and congresswoman from New York from 1971 to 1973, who became a close friend of Steinem's. She was involved with Women Strike for Peace.

DAVID BALE: The South African–born activist and businessman who married Steinem in 2000; he died in 2003.

ROBERT BENTON: The assistant art director at *Esquire* magazine who became one of Steinem's early partners; he became a screenwriter and director, winning Academy Awards for *Kramer vs. Kramer* and *Places in the Heart*.

PATRICIA CARBINE: Cofounder of *Ms.* magazine and long-term editor of the magazine.

CESAR CHAVEZ: Labor organizer for the United Farm Workers union.

SHIRLEY CHISHOLM: The first Black woman elected to the US House of Representatives, representing New York's Twelfth District from 1969 to 1983. In 1972, she became the first woman to run for the Democratic Party's presidential nomination. Chisholm cofounded the National Women's Political Caucus with Steinem and others.

BLAIR CHOTZINOFF: Steinem's fiancé during her senior year at Smith College.

BRENDA FEIGEN: Feminist organizer who cofounded the Women's Action Alliance with Steinem; *Ms.* magazine was an outgrowth of the alliance.

CLAY FELKER: The features editor at *Esquire* who gave Steinem her first serious assignment, about how birth control pills change women's behavior on college campuses; he became a lifelong friend and helped secure publication of the first issue of *Ms.* magazine.

BETTY FRIEDAN: Feminist author of the bestseller *The Feminine Mystique,* cofounder of the National Organization for Women (NOW), and a leader and participant in many women's rights causes.

KATHARINE GRAHAM: Publisher of the *Washington Post* and a feminist friend of Steinem's.

JANE GALVIN-LEWIS: Cofounder of the National Black Feminist Organization, writer for *Ms.* magazine, former deputy director of the Women's Action Alliance, who sometimes shared the stage with Steinem on her various speaking engagements.

CLIVE GRAY: A recruiter for the Central Intelligence Agency who met Steinem in India and later offered her a job with the Independent Research Service for the Vienna Youth Festival.

FANNIE LOU HAMER: Cofounder of the National Women's Political Caucus with Steinem and others; she was a leader in the civil rights movement.

BETTY HARRIS: A cofounder of *Ms.* magazine.

DOROTHY PITMAN HUGHES: Cofounder of the Women's Action Alliance in 1971 and *Ms.* magazine in 1972; she also toured with Steinem at speaking engagements throughout the 1970s. She organized the first shelter for women experiencing domestic violence in New York City and opened three childcare centers.

FLORYNCE "FLO" KENNEDY: Cofounder of the National Black Feminist Organization and the National Women's Political Caucus; she appeared in public appearances with Steinem throughout the 1970s. She graduated from Columbia Law School in 1951.

HARVEY KURTZMAN: The creator of *Mad* magazine who offered Steinem her first freelance writing job in New York at his magazine *Help! For Tired Minds*.

WILMA MANKILLER: Former chief of the Cherokee Nation and a close friend of Steinem's.

KATE MILLETT: Feminist writer and intellectual.

MARION MOSES: A nurse from the United Farm Workers union who worked with Steinem on behalf of the migrant laborers.

ELEANOR HOLMES NORTON: Cofounder of the National Black Feminist Organization and a civil rights activist. She was on the founding advisory board of the *Women's Rights Law Reporter*, the first legal periodical to focus on women's rights law. Since 1990 she has served as a nonvoting delegate to the United States House of Representatives, representing the District of Columbia.

JOSEPH NUNEVILLER: Gloria Steinem's maternal grandfather.

MARIE OCHS: Gloria Steinem's maternal grandmother; Steinem used her name when working undercover as a Playboy Bunny and when receiving treatment for breast cancer.

PAULINE PERLMUTTER: Gloria Steinem's paternal grandmother and a suffragist in Ohio.

HERB SARGENT: Another of Steinem's partners, who worked as a television writer and producer for *The Tonight Show* and *Saturday Night Live*, among others.

PHYLLIS SCHLAFLY: A conservative opponent of the Equal Rights Amendment.

MARGARET SLOAN-HUNTER: Editor and writer at *Ms.* magazine and cofounder of the National Black Feminist Organization.

JOSEPH STEINEM: Gloria Steinem's paternal grandfather.

LEO STEINEM: Gloria Steinem's father.

RUTH STEINEM: Gloria Steinem's mother.

SUSANNE STEINEM PATCH: Gloria Steinem's sister, who was nine years older.

ALICE WALKER: Author, feminist activist, former editor of *Ms.*, and close friend of Steinem's; she won the National Book Award and Pulitzer Prize for her novel *The Color Purple*.

REBECCA WALKER: Feminist writer and activist who published an article on feminism in 1992 in *Ms.* magazine declaring, "I am the Third Wave"; Steinem is her godmother and one of her mentors.

MORTIMER ZUCKERMAN: Billionaire real-estate developer, magazine editor, and investor, who was Steinem's partner in the mid-1980s.

BIBLIOGRAPHY

Associated Press. "David Bale, Gloria Steinem's Husband, Dies." *AP News*, January 1, 2004.

Attebury, Nancy Garhan. *Gloria Steinem: Champion of Women's Rights*. Minneapolis: Compass Point Books, 2006.

Bruk, Diana. "Here's the Full Transcript of Gloria Steinem's Historic Women's March Speech." *Elle*, January 21, 2017.

Carroll, Rebecca. "What I See: Gloria Steinem, Shoulder to Shoulder with Women of Color." *New York Times*, December 10, 2018.

Cooke, Rachel. "Gloria Steinem: 'I think we need to get much angrier.'" *Guardian* (US edition), November 12, 2011.

Darrough, Celia. "What Gloria Steinem Wants Women to Know About America's Obsession With Guns." *Bustle*, June 1, 2018.

Department of State. *". . . To Form a More Perfect Union . . .": Justice for American Women: Report of the National Commission on the Observance of International Women's Year*. Washington, DC, 1976.

Dullea, Georgia. "Birthday Celebration: Gloria Steinem at 50." *New York Times*, May 24, 1984.

Fabiny, Sarah. *Who Is Gloria Steinem?* New York: Grosset & Dunlap, 2014.

Farrell, Amy Erdman. *Yours in Sisterhood: Ms. Magazine and the Promise of Popular Feminism*. Chapel Hill: University of North Carolina Press, 1998.

Feminist Majority Foundation. *"Ms. Magazine and Feminist Majority Foundation Join Forces."* Press Release, November 12, 2001.

Friedan, Betty. *The Feminine Mystique*. New York: Norton, 1963.

———. *It Changed My Life: Writings on the Women's Movement*. New York: Random House, 1976.

———. *The Second Stage*. New York: Summit, 1981.

Green, Jesse. "Review: 'Gloria: A Life,' Starring Ms. Steinem and Her Audience." *New York Times*, October 18, 2018.

Gupta, Ruchira, ed. *The Essential Gloria Steinem Reader: As if Women Matter*. New Delhi, India: Rupa Publications, 2014.

Hass, Nancy. "Gloria Steinem: The Future of the Fight for Women's Rights." *Newsweek*, August 7, 2011.

Heilbrun, Carolyn G. *The Education of a Woman: The Life of Gloria Steinem*. New York: Dial Press, 1995.

Kahn, Mattie. "Gloria Steinem on Harvey Weinstein's Downfall, Hugh Hefner's Death, and the Patriarchy's Endless Last Gasp." *Elle*, October 12, 2017.

Karbo, Karen. *In Praise of Difficult Women: Life Lessons from 29 Heroines Who Dared to Break the Rules*. Washington, DC: National Geographic, 2018.

Kramer, Jane. "Road Warrior." *The New Yorker*, October 12, 2015.

Leland, John. "Showgirls, Pastrami and Candor: Gloria Steinem's New York." *New York Times*, October 7, 2016.

Levine, Suzanne Braun, and Mary Thom. *Bella Abzug: How One Tough Broad from the Bronx Fought Jim Crow and Joe McCarthy, Pissed Off Jimmy Carter, Battled for the Rights of Women and Workers, Rallied Against War and for the Planet, and Shook Up Politics Along the Way, An Oral History*. New York: Farrar, Straus and Giroux, 2007.

Los Angeles Times Staff; "Margaret Sloan-Hunter, 57; Writer Formed Black Feminist Organization." *Los Angeles Times*, October 15, 2004.

Morgan, Robin, ed. *Sisterhood Is Powerful: An Anthology of Writings from the Women's Liberation Movement*. New York: Random House, 1970.

——. *Sisterhood Is Global: The International Women's Movement Anthology*. Garden City, NY: Anchor Press/Doubleday, 1984.

Nemy, Enid. "They're Black, So Feminism Has Even More Obstacles Than Usual." *The New York Times*, November 7, 1973.

People Staff. "Gloria Steinem." *People*, December 25, 2000.

Pogrebin, Abigail. "How Do You Spell Ms." *New York*, October 28, 2011.

Starr, Penny. "Gloria Steinem Says Her Medal of Freedom Will Honor 'Work of Margaret Sanger." CNSNews.com, November 18, 2013.

Steinem, Gloria. *Doing Sixty & Seventy*. San Francisco: Elders Academy Press, 2006.

——; photographs by George Barris. *Marilyn: Norma Jean*. New York: Holt, 1986.

——. *Moving Beyond Words: Essays on Age, Rage, Sex, Power, Money, Muscles: Breaking Boundaries of Gender*. New York: Simon & Schuster, 1994.

——. *My Life on the Road*. New York: Random House, 2015.

——. *Outrageous Acts and Everyday Rebellions*. New York: Holt, Rinehart and Winston, 1983.

——. *Revolution from Within: A Book of Self-Esteem*. New York: Little Brown, 1992.

Stern, Sydney Ladensohn. *Gloria Steinem: Her Passions, Politics, and Mystique*. Secaucus, NJ: Carol Publishing Group, 1997.

Sheila Stogsdill, "Gloria Steinem reflects on friendship with Wilma Mankiller," *Oklahoman*, April 8, 2010, https://oklahoman.com/article/3452255/gloria-stienem-reflects-on-friendship -with-wilma-mankiller.

Thom, Mary. *Inside Ms.: 25 Years of the Magazine and the Feminist Movement*. New York: Henry Holt, 1997.

——, ed. *Letters to Ms. 1972–1987*. New York: Henry Holt, 1987.

Von Zielbauer, Paul. "David Bale, 62, Activist and Businessman." *New York Times*, January 1, 2004.

"Walters Interviews Gloria Steinem," interview by Barbara Walters. *ABC News*, April 18, 2001.

Wheaton, Elizabeth. *Ms.: The Story of Gloria Steinem*. Greensboro, NC: Morgan Reynolds, 2002.

Zernike, Kate. "Rutgers to Endow Chair Named for Gloria Steinem." *New York Times*, September 26, 2014.

"Yes 'Way' for *Ms.* magazine! Mendez, Steinem and Co. unveil new street sign." *The Villager*, November 30, 2017. https://www.thevillager.com/2017/11/yes-way-for-ms-magazine-mendez -steinem-and-co-unveil-new-street-sign/.

The *Ms.* archives are housed at the Sophia Smith Collection at Smith College, Northampton, Massachusetts.

SOURCE NOTES

CHAPTER 1: ALMOST

"Once you get a taste of being
independent . . .": Stern, 87.

"a little death . . .": Stern, 85.

"I loved him and cared about him . . .":
Stern, 85.

"It's probably a good idea . . .": Stern, 87.

CHAPTER 2: AN UNTRADITIONAL CHILDHOOD

"We were loved and valued . . .": Garhan, 22.

"I believe in woman suffrage . . .": Stern, 9.

"differentiated only by the outer
garments . . .": Stern, 9.

"They walked around in the snow . . .":
Heilbrun, 5.

"Let's get married . . .": Heilbrun, 10.

"To My First Wife": Heilbrun, 10.

"the best-paid job on the paper . . .":
Wheaton, 13.

"over the water, under the stars": Stern, 14.

"a resort worthy of the big dance bands . . .":
Wheaton, 13.

"breaking point": Wheaton, 15.

"From now on, I'm going with you . . .":
Wheaton, 15.

"a great time of running wild . . .":
Heilbrun, 16.

"My father often had to park . . .": Heilbrun, 17.

"Louisa May Alcott was my friend . . .":
Wheaton, 17.

"I don't believe I shall ever marry . . .":
Stern, 27.

"He taught me routines . . .": Heilbrun, 20.

"I loved sitting there . . .": Heilbrun, 20.

"He treated me like a friend . . .": Heilbrun, 20.

"Against all he had been taught . . .":
Heilbrun, 20–21.

"Over and over again, in every way . . .":
Attebury, 22.

CHAPTER 3: ON THEIR OWN

"I knew that my mother loved me . . .":
Heilbrun, 24.

"Between visits he sent postcards . . .":
Steinem, *My Life*, 11.

"Class was very important to me . . .":
Attebury, 31.

"Though I loved my parents . . .":
Attebury, 26.

"I knew that my mother loved me . . .":
Heilbrun, 24.

"For many years . . .": Steinem, *Outrageous
Acts*, 140.

"I remember so well the dread . . .":
Wheaton, 21.

"Humiliated in front of my friends . . .":
Attebury, 30.

"How can I travel . . .": Stern, 38.

"At home it felt dangerous . . .": Stern, 43.

"The house was in a bad state . . .":
Heilbrun, 25.

CHAPTER 4: SENIOR YEAR

"One year is all . . .": Wheaton, 23.
"No, we're divorced . . .": Stern, 54.
"All right . . .": Wheaton, 23.
"We are sisters . . .": Heilbrun, 35.

CHAPTER 5: SMITH

"Don't worry about your background . . .":
    Wheaton, 25.
"with a name like Steinem . . .": Stern, 65.
"I took geology . . .": Stern, 68.
"What do you mean 'easily'?": Stern, 69–70.
"Don't worry about your background . . .":
    Wheaton, 25.
"We've just finished washing . . .":
    Heilbrun, 47.
"Why study three extra years . . .":
    Wheaton, 26.

CHAPTER 6: ABORTION

"I couldn't admit that I was the one . . .":
    Stern, 94.
"you didn't *necessarily* die": Stern, 94.
"I told him a long story . . .": Stern, 94.
"she promise to do what she really
    wanted . . .": Wheaton, 28.
"the first time I stopped passively . . .":
    Heilbrun, 69.
"My own [abortion] had taken place . . .":
    Heilbrun, 69.

CHAPTER 7: INDIA

"Most of us have a few events . . .":
    Wheaton, 30.
"How will I ever . . .": Stern, 101.
"be respected as one . . .": Wheaton, 29.
"He literally turned the hierarchy . . .":
    Heilbrun, 73.
"I found there was a freedom . . .": Stern, 104.
"Each day, we set off along paths . . .": Stern,
    104.
"There were so many stories . . .":
    Wheaton, 30.

"Every great social justice movement . . .":
    Kahn.
"if we get together . . .": Kahn.
"If you do something the people . . .":
    Wheaton, 30.
"Most of us have a few events . . .":
    Wheaton, 30.
"In a windowless Las Vegas casino . . .":
    Steinem, *Road*, 16.
"It was the same technique . . .": Steinem,
    Road, 16.

CHAPTER 8: THE CIA CONNECTION

"I was mostly trying to earn a living.":
    Stern, 160.
"If I brought up India . . .": Stern, 107.
"I'm afraid the idealism . . .": Stern, 160.
"remembers feeling relief . . .":
    Wheaton, 34.

CHAPTER 9: LEO'S DEATH

"The cars are coming too fast to stop.":
    Steinem, *Road*, 16.
"If we're ever in an accident . . .": Steinem,
    Road, 16.
"I think I sensed . . .": Steinem, *Road*,
    17.
"When I arrived at the hospital . . .":
    Steinem, *Road*, 17.
"I will never stop wishing . . .": Steinem,
    Road, 18.
"If I don't know . . .": Steinem, *Road*, 19.
"'That's okay,' he said . . .": Steinem, *Road*,
    22.
"Only after I saw women . . .": Steinem,
    Road, 22–23.
"Your father saved the summer . . .":
    Steinem, *Road*, 24.
"My father knew a good heart . . .": Steinem,
    Road, 25.
"I wish I could remember . . .": Steinem,
    Road, 27.

CHAPTER 10: FREELANCE WRITER

"For me, writing is the only thing . . .":
    Wheaton, p. 36.
"Congratulations. You've managed . . .":
    Stern, 131.
"Blair was a kind, sexual, sensual . . .":
    Stern, 123.
"It wasn't just compromise . . .": Stern, 126.
"The first was to do the blood tests . . .":
    Kramer.

CHAPTER 11: BUNNY

"All women are Bunnies.": Steinem,
    Outrageous, 75.
"Do Playboy Club . . .": Steinem,
    Outrageous, 32.
"It sounds much too square . . .": Steinem,
    Outrageous, 33.
"I went, and the thing took on . . ."
    Heilbrun, 105.
"wardrobe mistress": Steinem,
    Outrageous, 37.
"It was so tight that the zipper . . .":
    Steinem, *Outrageous*, 38.
"The whole costume was darted . . .":
    Steinem, *Outrageous*, 40.
"The costume was so tight . . .": Cooke.
"Is that required of waitresses . . .": Steinem,
    Outrageous, 46.
"I went back to the Bunny room . . .":
    Steinem, *Outrageous*, 56.
"The men called colored girls . . .":
    Heilbrun, 106.
"Somehow, the usual tail-pullings . . .":
    Wheaton, 44.
"Dear Miss Steinem . . .": Heilbrun, 107.
"I'm afraid I can't . . .": Heilbrun, 107–108.
"That piece put you on the map.":
    Stern, 139.
"After feminism arrived in my life . . .":
    Steinem, *Outrageous*, 75.
"all women are Bunnies," Steinem,
    Outrageous, 75.

CHAPTER 12: OUTSIDER

"*I'll definitely get married* . . .": Wheaton,
    45–46.
"There are people who know me . . .":
    Stern, 151.
"Usually the journalist remembers his
    place . . .": Heilbrun, 126.
"Steinem: Easier than you think.":
    Heilbrun, 127.
"Who's Who of the World":
    Stern, 149.
"Miss Steinem swings with the new
    society . . .": Stern, 155.
"It's amazing how fast . . .":
    Stern, 134
"trying on the name and life . . .":
    Wheaton, 45.
"[I] thought I would *have* to marry . . .":
    Wheaton, 45–46.
"I used to seek out rich and famous
    men . . .": Stern, 185.

CHAPTER 13: COLUMNIST

"For the first time . . .": Attebury, 49.
"You know how every year . . .":
    Kramer.
CHILDREN ARE NOT FOR BURNING: Levine and
    Thom, *Bella Abzug*, 69.
"Bella was leading the presentation . . .":
    Levine and Thom, *Bella Abzug*, 69.
"I will oppose the war . . .": Levine and
    Thom, *Bella Abzug*, 69.
"I had never seen a woman . . .": Levine and
    Thom, *Bella Abzug*, 70.
"For the first time . . .": Attebury, 49.
"What are you doing . . .": Stern, 161.
"Like other women, I had either stayed . . .":
    Attebury, 51.
"George McGovern is the real Eugene
    McCarthy.": Stern, 163.
"I was distributing literature . . ."
    Stern, 165.
"No broads": Stern, 166.

CHAPTER 14: UNITED FARM WORKERS

"There are few rewards greater . . .":
Steinem, *Road*, 216.

"Right away Marion's sense of urgency . . .":
Steinem, *Road*, 217.

"I felt like an idiot . . .": Steinem, *Road*, 217.

"Honey, I'd like to press your grapes!":
Steinem, *Road*, 217–18.

"whenever I can": Heilbrun, 151.

"barbarians": Heilbrun, 151.

"Farmworkers from Mexico . . .": Steinem,
Road, 215.

"This historic event . . .": Steinem,
Road, 215.

"I'm surprised by how much . . .": Steinem,
Road, 216.

CHAPTER 15: FEMINIST AWAKENING

"Once the light began to dawn . . .":
Wheaton, 60.

"husband's wife, children's mother . . .":
Stern, 193.

"I shared the reaction . . .": Wheaton, 40.

"unescorted ladies": Wheaton, 54.

"I was humiliated . . .": Wheaton, 54.

"I called my subject . . .": Wheaton, 55.

"When I faced the hotel manager . . .":
Wheaton, 55.

"Feminist ideas began to explode . . .":
Wheaton, 48–49.

"You get into a car . . .": Stern, 188.

"the great blinding light bulb":
Heilbrun, 170.

"I had had an abortion . . .": Wheaton, 59.

"I researched as much as I could . . .":
Heilbrun, 172.

"a long-lasting and important . . .":
Wheaton, 61.

"It is truly amazing how long . . .":
Wheaton, 60.

CHAPTER 16: FINDING HER VOICE

"I would have remained silent . . .": Steinem,
Outrageous, 13.

"as relentlessly second class . . .":
Wheaton, 65.

"irrelevant, unstimulating, and
demeaning . . .": Stern, 214.

"Any change is fearful . . .":
Wheaton, 65.

"We do want to change . . .": Wheaton,
65–66.

"There seems to be no punishment . . .":
Wheaton, 54.

"The very idea of speaking to a group . . .":
Steinem, *Outrageous*, 12.

"In the past when magazines . . .": Steinem,
Outrageous, 12.

"I would have remained silent . . .": Steinem,
Outrageous, 13.

"Right away we discovered that
a white woman . . .": Steinem,
Road, 47.

"She would nurse the baby . . .": Thom,
Inside Ms., 7.

"If you have admitted any white man . . .":
Stern, 206.

"Glo-ball": Stern, 207.

"It was Flo especially . . .": Steinem,
Outrageous, 12.

"Flo also rescued me . . .": Steinem,
Outrageous, 12.

"Nobody ever talks . . .": Stern, 209.

"Are you my alternative?":
Heilbrun, 204.

"It disclosed nothing, confused the
accuser . . .": Steinem, *Road*, 51.

"Though we tried to focus . . .": Steinem,
Road, 204.

"Years of getting up . . .": Steinem,
Outrageous, 13.

"A mutual understanding comes . . .":
Steinem, *Outrageous*, 13–14.

CHAPTER 17: FEMINIST FEUD

"The media tried to make her a celebrity . . .": Stern, 257.

"lavender menace": Steinem, *Road*, 60.

"Kate Millett herself . . .": Stern, 218.

"a society free from defining . . .": Stern, 219.

"Monosexual. It sounds so boring.": Stern, 220.

"most effective spokeswoman and symbol": Stern, 226.

"She is, in short, a transitional figure . . .": Stern, 226.

"This was especially clear to me . . .": Wheaton, 75.

"the intellectuals' pinup": Stern, 230.

"This woman, who advanced . . .": Stern, 230.

"I often grew cross . . .": Wheaton, 69.

"Mother Superior of Women's Lib": Wheaton, 83.

"Let me say to you . . .": Wheaton, 196.

"there are only a few jobs . . .": Wheaton, 196.

"a five- or ten-thousand-year-old . . .": Stern, 256.

"With homemakers having . . .": Stern, 256.

"female chauvinist boors": Stern, 258.

"the princess among the grape pickers": Stern, 226.

"never been part . . .": Stern, 257.

"Gloria has not advanced . . .": Heilbrun, 192.

"The media tried to make her a celebrity . . .": Stern, 257.

"I never responded . . .": Steinem, *Road*, 152.

"ripping off the movement . . .": Stern, 257.

"no feud between Gloria and me": Stern, 257.

"Don't do anything . . .": Heilbrun, 272.

"It's the practice . . .": Heilbrun, 272.

CHAPTER 18: THE NATIONAL WOMEN'S POLITICAL CAUCUS

"At that Democratic Convention . . .": Steinem, *Road*, 150.

"I feel our obligation . . .": Stern, 237.

"a white, male, middle-class . . .": Steinem, *Road*, 151–52.

"every woman whose abilities . . .": Stern, 239.

"Once chapters were established . . .": Steinem, *Road*, 150.

"Between July, when the caucus was founded . . .": Levine, 143.

"Unfortunately, as I learned . . .": Steinem, *Road*, 151.

"There was a strong women's plank . . .": Steinem, *Road*, 153.

"At that Democratic Convention . . .": Steinem, *Road*, 150.

"The Democratic Party . . .": Steinem, *Outrageous*, 115.

"wept with rage": Heilbrun, 236.

"I cry when I get angry.": Heilbrun, 236.

"The right to reproductive freedom . . .": Steinem, *Outrageous*, 116.

"It was the first time . . .": Steinem, *Road*, 153.

"I'm for Shirley Chisholm . . .": Heilbrun, 238.

"Shirley's mere presence . . .": Steinem, *Road*, 153.

"Women are never again . . .": Steinem, *Outrageous*, 120.

CHAPTER 19: THE EQUAL RIGHTS AMENDMENT

"Equality of rights . . .": Attebury, 60–61.

"I have been denied . . .": Attebury, 62.

"*States' rights* and *local legislative control* . . .": Steinem, *Outrageous*, 376.

"To my knowledge . . .": Steinem, *Outrageous*, 356.

"In the early days of the civil rights movement . . .": Steinem, *Outrageous*, 358.

"Feminists began draft-based . . .": Steinem, *Outrageous*, 362–63.

"The point of feminism . . .": Steinem, *Outrageous*, 365.

"Speaking got easier . . .": Stern, 331.

"One inevitable result . . ." Steinem, *Outrageous*, 373.

CHAPTER 20: PREVIEW

"*Ms.* is a magazine . . .": Stern, 261.

"obviously intelligent, glamorous woman . . .": Heilbrun, 207.

"This was [my] first realization . . .": Heilbrun, 207.

"You're already too well-known . . .": Stern, 262.

"*For a Better World*": Farrell, 60.

"*Ms.* is a magazine . . .": Stern, 261.

"People said we shouldn't . . .": Stern, 275.

"*Ms.* is written for all women . . .": Farrell, 72.

CHAPTER 21: MS.

"I remembered many, many women . . .": Wheaton, 77.

"We had problems . . .": Steinem, *Beyond Words*, 136.

"I remember we sat around . . .": Stern, 269.

"I'll give it six months . . .": Stern, 81.

"C-sharp on an untuned piano . . .": Stern, 81.

"anti-family, anti-children . . .": Farrell, 51.

"I wanted there to be a feminist magazine . . .": Heilbrun, 231.

CHAPTER 22: ADVERTISING

"Over the years . . .": Steinem, *Beyond Words*, 135.

"respect[ed] women's judgment . . .": Farrell, 30.

"When *Ms.* began . . .": Steinem, *Beyond Words*, 132.

"If *Ms.* could prove that women . . .": Steinem, *Beyond Words*, 132.

"Carmakers were still draping . . .": Steinem, *Beyond Words*, 134.

"complementary copy": Stern, 279.

"Publishing ads only . . .": Steinem, *Beyond Words*, 133.

"hostile editorial environment": Stern, 279.

"I wouldn't buy a page . . .": Stern, 280.

"If Mommy had worn a Bulova . . .": Stern, 280–81.

CHAPTER 23: CIA BACKLASH

"I took no orders . . .": Stern, 302.

"I'm fine . . .": Stern, 291.

"Far from being shocked . . .": Stern, 292.

"wanted to do what we wanted . . .": Stern, 292.

"Gloria Steinem has a ten-year association . . .": Wheaton, 88.

"watered down": Stern, 293.

"because of its pressing importance": Stern, 295.

WELCOME TO THE CIA: Stern, 298.

"been watching for years . . .": Stern, 294.

"Trashing is a particularly vicious . . .": Stern, 294.

CHAPTER 24: HOUSTON

"It was the most racially, economically . . .": Levine, 196.

"The contagion of feminism . . .": Farrell, 71–72.

"It was a constitutional convention . . .": Steinem, *Road*, 54.

"I was as scared . . .": Steinem, *Road*, 55.

"These state conferences were part . . .": Levine, 198.

"I began to see that for some . . .": Steinem, *Road*, 57.

"The Commission on International Women's Year . . .": Levine, 206.

"With issue areas from the arts . . .": Steinem, *Road*, 58.

"Across town, a right-wing . . .": Steinem, *Road*, 58.

"In the midst of this chaos . . .": Steinem, *Road*, 59.

"This was an honor . . .": Steinem, *Road*, 61–62.

"For the first time, minority women . . .": Heilbrun, 318.

"Somehow, this all had to go . . .": Steinem, *Road*, 62.

"I began to realize . . .": Steinem, *Road*, 63.

"Let this message go forth . . .": Steinem, *Road*, 65.

"It was the high point . . .": Steinem, *Road*, 65.

"I saw a white man . . .": Steinem, *Road*, 65.

"I was surprised to find myself . . .": Steinem, *Road*, 65.

"I wore the necklace . . .": Steinem, *Road*, 66–67.

"It may take the prize . . .": Steinem, *Road*, 53–54.

CHAPTER 25: OUTSPOKEN

"Glory be to God for Gloria!": Steinem, *Road*, 203–04.

"He himself prays . . .": Steinem, *Road*, 207.

"I'm worried about getting him . . .": Steinem, *Road*, 203.

"Gloria Steinem is a murderer . . .": Steinem, *Road*, 203.

"Father Egan tells me . . .": Steinem, *Road*, 203.

"I am not suggesting to you . . .": Heilbrun, 333.

"If we listen only to people . . .": Heilbrun, 333.

"Nothing in my life . . .": Steinem, *Road*, 206.

"a Sunday presentation": Steinem, *Road*, 206.

CHAPTER 26: STATUS CHANGES

"*Ms.* is the exception . . .": Farrell, 111.

"This new status . . ." Farrell, 111.

"*Ms.* would be rated 'X' . . .": Stern, 286.

"I was at fault . . .": Stern, 356.

"Having for the first time . . .": Heilbrun, 363.

"I felt I was walking on eggs . . .": Heilbrun, 369.

CHAPTER 27: GOODBYE, RUTH

"Dying seems less sad . . .": Steinem, *Outrageous*, 158.

"tell them that this . . .": Wheaton, 87.

"I do occasionally bask . . .": Stern, 332.

"I remember sitting at my old . . .": Heilbrun, 343–44.

"I miss her . . ." Steinem, *Outrageous*, 158.

CHAPTER 28: OUTRAGEOUS

"What outrageous act will I do today?": Steinem, *Outrageous*, 335.

"Any male writer my age . . .": Stern, 326.

"women's point of view": Heilbrun, 329.

"I have nightmares . . .": Heilbrun, 326.

"If each person in the room . . .": Stern, 335.

"I still don't understand . . .": Steinem, *Outrageous*, 155.

"While she was alive . . .": Wheaton, 92–93.

"Couldn't they at least say . . .": Steinem, *Outrageous*, 152.

"They could not identify . . .": Steinem, *Outrageous*, 151.

"Would you say . . .": Steinem, *Outrageous*, 151.

"At least we're now asking . . .": Steinem, *Outrageous*, 158.

"Since I understand this discomfort . . .":
 Steinem, *Outrageous*, 133.
"THE SECOND WAVE . . .":
 Heilbrun, 199.
"With alarmingly little spine . . .": Steinem,
 Outrageous, 135.
"It was all hushed up . . .": Steinem,
 Outrageous, 135.
"When we finally passed . . .": Steinem,
 Outrageous, 135–36.
"Sometimes people confuse . . .": Stern, 340.
"Well, it maybe was not . . .": Stern, 340.
"You don't look forty . . .": Stern, 341.
"a dashing role model . . .": Stern, 344.
"younger, thinner, and blonder than ever":
 Dullea.
"doing so many things . . .": Stern, 344.
"I think women can learn . . .": Stern, 360.
"The lifestyle and relatives . . .": Stern, 361.
"The restriction of her spirit . . .":
 Heilbrun, 375.
"We are all brothers . . .": Steinem,
 Outrageous, p. 259.
"We are too late . . .": Steinem,
 Outrageous, 261.
"Now that women's self-vision . . .":
 Steinem, *Outrageous*, 260.
"We'd been living . . .": Stern, 362.
"sheltered by a strong and timeless tree":
 Steinem, *Road*, 258.
"Just being with her . . .": Steinem, *Road*, 258.
"Only sitting in a circle . . .": Steinem,
 Road, 262.
"From then on, I realized . . .": Steinem,
 Road, 262.
"This is the first time in my life . . .":
 Steinem, *Road*, 262.

CHAPTER 29: CANCER
"I've had a good life.": Stern, 365.
"Not bad.": Stern, 364.
"gave me a little Novocain . . .": Stern, 365.

"If there is one thing . . .": Heilbrun, 378.
"How interesting . . .": Stern, 365.
"Such acceptance may sound odd . . .":
 Steinem, *Revolution*, 245.
"It was all right . . .": Stern, 365.
"Since the [lymph-node] sampling . . .":
 Stern, 245.
"I was frightened enough . . .": Stern,
 245–46.
"one of the rewards . . ." Stern, 246.
"It was Gloria who went with me . . .":
 Stern, 437.
"What's wrong with you . . .": Stern, 437.
"She just kept bothering me . . .": Stern, 438.

CHAPTER 30: SELLING AND BUYING *MS.*
"*Ms.* has found a new way . . .": Steinem,
 Beyond Words, 152.
"It's very sad . . ." Steinem, *Beyond
 Words*, 150.
"That's not in the spirit . . .": Stern, 372.
"The idea of having no ads . . .": Steinem,
 Beyond Words, 151.
"*Ms.* has found a new way . . .": Steinem,
 Beyond Words, 152.
"The magazine, despite its flaws . . .":
 Pogrebin.

CHAPTER 31: REFLECTION AND REVOLUTION
"I, who had spent . . .": Steinem,
 Revolution, 3.
"write what we need to know": Stern, 360.
"I had been repeating . . .": Steinem,
 Revolution, 7.
"The truth was that I had internalized . . .":
 Steinem, *Revolution*, 25.
"Studies show that low self-esteem . . .":
 Steinem, *Revolution*, 12.
"poured out like molasses": Steinem,
 Revolution, 159.

"It was odd to discover . . .": Steinem, *Revolution*, 160.

"I thought I had built . . .": Steinem, *Revolution*, 34.

"There was this thin . . .": Steinem, *Revolution*, 227.

"The idea for this book . . .": Steinem, *Revolution*, 3.

"I don't know how to tell . . .": Steinem, *Revolution*, 5.

"Why would anyone . . .": Stern, 380.

"I'm still trying to thread . . .": Steinem, *Revolution*, 387.

"I am his daughter . . .": Stern, 387.

"squishy exercise in feeling better": Steinem, *Revolution*, 329.

"I began to wonder . . .": Steinem, *Revolution*, 330.

"If I wasn't immune . . .": Steinem, *Revolution*, 338.

CHAPTER 32: AGING

"More and more . . .": Stern, 407–08.

"She was in a park . . .": Wheaton, 97.

"I was going to live . . .": Wheaton, 97.

"The central years of adulthood . . .": Steinem, *Sixty & Seventy*, vii.

"I've come to realize . . .": Steinem, *Sixty & Seventy*, vii.

"I'm looking forward . . .": Steinem, *Sixty & Seventy*, 407–08.

"I used to walk around . . .": Stern, 423.

"Home is a symbol . . .": Steinem, *Road*, 281.

"I always thought of myself . . .": Stern, 424.

"For many years I was jealous . . .": Stern, 424.

"moral compass": Stern, 428.

"Alice Walker is someone in my life . . .": Stern, 428.

"surrogate daughters": Heilbrun, 409.

"She was my champion . . .": Heilbrun, 411.

"I also felt that it created . . .": Heilbrun, 411.

"She's crystallized the emotions . . .": Stern, 439.

"Ten Surefire Tips . . .": Stern, 439.

"newness stretches out our experience . . .": Stern, xvii.

"Each day, I thought . . .": Wheaton, 98.

CHAPTER 33: MARRIAGE

"I couldn't imagine why I would . . .": *People*.

"Those amazing brown eyes . . .": *People*.

"Read this woman . . .": *People*.

"We're calling it a 'partnership'": Wheaton, 98.

"I did not change . . .": Attebury, 89.

"Thirty years of the women's movement . . .": Wheaton, 98.

"I hope this proves . . .": Wheaton, 99.

"There was no use of words . . .": *People*.

"I couldn't imagine . . .": *People*.

"marriage felt like a restriction . . .": *People*.

"Being married is like having . . .": *People*.

"We wouldn't have got married . . .": Cooke.

"You become a semi-nonperson . . .": "Walters Interviews."

"Because we both felt . . .": "Walters Interviews."

"David went through the world . . .": Associated Press.

"needed someone to help him out of life . . .": Kramer.

"It was terrible, terrible . . .": Cooke.

"It was actually very good for me . . .": Hass.

"Despite the shortness . . .": Steinem, *Sixty & Seventy*, xxi.

CHAPTER 34: BEYOND

"I'm using my torch . . .": Leland.

"In my first days of feminism . . .": Fabiny, 100.

"Even if we're no longer trying . . .": Stern, 444.

"To me, the idea that . . .": Stern, 443.

"I'd been submerging myself . . .": Steinem,
    Sixty & Seventy, 18.

"The need to treat ourselves . . .": Steinem,
    Sixty & Seventy, 19.

"Fifty was hardest for me . . .": Leland.

"This is an outpouring . . ." Bruk.

"I hope to live to one hundred . . .": Cooke.

"If you work on a campaign . . .": Kramer.

"In that case . . .": Darrough.

"Guns are related to masculinity . . ."
    Darrough.

"Men who are guilty of domestic
    violence . . ." Darrough.

"We were a chosen family," Stogsdill.

"This worldview has more layers . . .":
    Steinem, *On the Road*, 271.

"Wilma just seemed to pull away . . ."
    Steinem, *On the Road*, 271.

"The moment after . . ." Steinem, *On the
    Road*, 278.

"I once asked Wilma . . ." Steinem, *On the
    Road*, 280.

"My funeral will be a fund-raiser," Leland.

"People are always asking . . .": Fabiny, 100.

BOX: PARTNERS IN JUSTICE

"the double discrimination . . .": Steinem,
    Road, 109.

BOX: THE MS. FOUNDATION

"Take Your Daughter Home": Stern, 314.

"There's no Take Our Sons . . .": Stern, 314.

INDEX